REJOICING IN THE TRUTH

Rejoicing in the Truth

WISDOM AND

THE EDUCATOR'S CRAFT

Christopher O. Blum

Christendom Press
2015

Blum, Christopher Olaf, 1969-

    Rejoicing in the truth : wisdom and the educator's craft / Christopher O. Blum. — Front Royal, VA : Christendom Press, 2015.

    pages ; cm.

        ISBN: 978-0-931888-85-4
        Includes bibliographical references and index.
        Summary: A vision for the renewal of Christian education through the intentional pursuit of wisdom. When educators make it their goal to accompany their students along the path to wisdom and to instruct them by showing them how to delight in the truth, then their practice is illuminated and enlivened at every level. Informed by the philosophical and theological visions of John Henry Newman, John Paul II, Alasdair MacIntyre, and Thomas Aquinas, this volume offers a series of different looks at the life of a Christian educator.—Publisher.

        1. Christian education. 2. Christian education—Philosophy. 3. Christian educators. 4. Christian scholars. 5. Learning and scholarship. 6. Wisdom—Religious aspects—Christianity. 7. Truth—Religious aspects—Christianity. 8. Intellectual life—Religious aspects—Christianity. I. Title.

BV1471.3 .B58 2015
268—dc23   1509

Published in the United States by:
Christendom Press
www.christendom.edu/press

Cover image: Return of the Prodigal Son *(1670), Bartolome Esteban Murillo*
Cover design by Kelly Cole

Manufactured in the United States of America

Contents

Foreword

WHEN DANTE DESCRIBED THE unique importance of adolescent education he insisted on an essential encounter with the qualities of awe, modesty, and shame, for he said that "all three are necessary at this age for the following reasons: at this age it is necessary to feel reverence and a desire for wisdom; at this age it is necessary to be under control so as not to transgress; at this age it is necessary to be penitent for a fault so as not to fall in the habit of committing it." These qualities were then necessary in themselves, but particularly so at this age for they were the preconditions not only for friendship but also for that nobility of soul, that beatitude which is the end of human life. And Dante suggests that if these qualities are not developed at this critical stage of life, they are unlikely to be developed at all. But as Christopher Blum notes, this great tradition of education on which Dante drew has been compromised by a variety of modern assumptions that have reduced education to a mere technique, a reduction with catastrophic consequences.

These reflections on the current dilemmas and necessary reforms of Catholic education are written with the elegance and sharp insight that place them within the highest tradition of the essay. They are the product of patient and penetrating contemplation and provide a remarkable reconsideration of the task of wisdom and of the ideologies that have obscured it in our time.

Blum first stresses the implications of the loss of a personal relation with nature, of that basic experience of observing its complex rhythms and varied operations. This is not without consequences for the basic ability to experience things directly for we have lost a formation of mind that might allow us to look at natural reality and to experience it first hand. He cites a recent British study that concluded that eight year olds were more likely to be able to identify characters in a Pokemon game than native species in the area in which they lived. This is surely not accidental, for society as a whole is now marked by a saturation of impressions and technologies that overwhelm the imagination.

What Dante described as awe, that "bewilderment of the mind at seeing and hearing great things," Aquinas had earlier described as *admiratio*, that sense of wonder at the recognition of the ordering of things to their ultimate end, which is God. Blum reminds us that for Aquinas, "Every science and art is ordered to one [end], namely, to the perfection of man, which is his beatitude." This we know instinctively, Blum notes, for "we do not admire random occurrences; we are frightened by them." But this recognition of the metaphysical foundations of all education, the desire to contemplate the origin, relations, and ends of things, has been set aside in favor of what Aquinas called the vice of curiosity, a vice which can rightly be contrasted with the virtue of studiousness. For studiousness, he said, consists in intellectual restraint. For Aquinas, the task of study is to curb the desire for knowledge, at least of that knowledge which is unintegrated and thus disordered, or what Newman called mere information.

But the Enlightenment stressed the central importance of encyclopedic knowledge, a restless pursuit of new knowledge, a restlessness that now becomes the criterion of the modern intellectual seeker, for as Montaigne had stressed, "When the mind is satisfied, that is a sign of diminished faculties or weariness." The mind is not called to rest in the truth and contemplate its mysteries but to extend its range. In the new encyclopedic tradition, Blum notes, "all truths are equal; their only order is alphabetical." Such a tradition will inevitably stress the importance of expertise in increasingly specialized fields and will condemn as irrelevant or obscurantist any attempt to situate the new knowledge in any organic relation to other truths or organizing principles or ends.

Blum's experience has largely been within higher education, but he is right to note that the various pathologies he describes in the modern university inevitably influence secondary education in their turn. How then might one create the conditions for renewing an education ordered to the end of wisdom and the knowledge of God? On the one hand, most fundamentally, one must turn decisively to the great teacher, the Logos, Jesus Christ. But in the Catholic tradition, one encounters as well a great cloud of witnesses, among whom Blum mentions explicitly John Paul II, Thérèse of Lisieux, John Henry Newman, Teresa of Avila, Aquinas, Augustine, and Benedict XVI. Each of these figures, four of them Doctors of the Church, provide fundamentally important historical insights about the nature and ends of education and its relation to wonder, that joy in the truth for which we were made.

In concluding, Blum considers the insights of two modern philosophers of education, Newman and Alasdair MacIntyre, whose reflections on the roles of faith and reason and the unity of knowledge draw upon the rich sources of the Catholic intellectual tradition and provide a contemporary translation of their significance. In the *Idea of a University*, Newman had argued that the university's task was to form an integrated habit of mind in its students, a philosophical habit which would enable them to see things in relation, to make judgments about the complex realities they would confront in life. In order to achieve this intellectual end, the university would require the assistance of the Church, an assistance that would itself serve the intellectual aims of the university. For without it, the university would tend in the direction of the fragmentation of the circle of knowledge and the compartmentalization of its offices. MacIntyre has drawn heavily on Newman in recent years, confirming his diagnosis of the dangers inherent in the substitution of the ends of power or sentiment for the integrative task of liberal education.

In this compelling work, Blum offers not only a clear and balanced assessment of the reductionist educational pathologies we now confront but, perhaps more important for our time, he provides a guide for the perplexed, a reassessment of the nature and promise of a classical Catholic humanistic education. He explores the roles of literature, history, and biology within that tradition and includes an engaging and insightful reflection on the importance of Euclidian geometry. In doing so he offers a way into the renewal of Catholic education, a renewal which would once again offer the promise of forming an essential habit of mind ,which necessarily includes forming habits of observation, of learning once again to look at nature, habits of reflection in experiencing the great texts of the tradition, habits of study in which students might establish a more disciplined and free approach to the truth, habits of prayer and devotion that will orient students more fully and existentially to the ultimate truth of God and of their own lives, habits of friendship made possible in a community of conviction and contemplation which binds students and teachers together in a common purpose and commitment.

These reflections, at once deeply personal and intensely scholarly, provide an essential foundation and an indispensable guide for the retrieval and renewal of Catholic education and Catholic culture.

— Don J. Briel

Preface

THE CATHOLIC TRADITION IS a quenchless source of renewal for the educator's craft. This renewal is not only a perpetual necessity, but a pressing current one. For although the last half-century of Catholic education has seen many generous and creative works, it has also witnessed significant betrayals of Catholic identity, strayings from the path of wisdom, and, in some places, a growing fatigue. This state of affairs is an unsatisfactory one, especially in light of the high ideal that has characterized the Christian intellectual life through the ages, the ideal of rejoicing in the truth (cf. 1 Cor. 13:6). No one scholar and teacher can address all of the challenges that beset Catholic education in this new century. Nevertheless, these essays on the pursuit of wisdom are offered in the hope that they might help to spark efforts of renovation and renewal.

This volume arises from the practice of collegiate teaching, yet it should also find a sympathetic audience in teachers and administrators at secondary schools. It is an indisputable fact that where colleges and universities go, high schools and middle schools soon follow. This trend seems typically to work for ill, as it has in our public schools, but it can work for good, as the growth and spread of alternative Christian and Classical schools over the past generation surely demonstrate. For every one renewed Catholic or Christian college, there are dozens of schools and home-school cooperatives staffed by its graduates, men and women who have dedicated themselves to the high task of ordering their work by wisdom.

Yet in order to attain wisdom, we must first desire it as our goal, and to do that, we must know something of what it is. Here faith comes to our aid, and proposes for our instruction the lives of the saints. John Paul II, Thérèse of Lisieux, John Henry Newman, Theresa of Avila, Aquinas, Augustine, and so many others: we profit from a cloud of witnesses who show us the path that ascends to the knowledge of God. We ought to be confident that the path taken by the saints is one that we too can follow. To do so, we must first take an honest look at our own intellectual habits, which have been deeply wounded by the vice of curiosity. Accordingly, the first chapter of this book attempts that appraisal with the help of Aquinas's treatment of curiosity. Then we must have a vision of what would be a healthy condition of mind, so that we might take steps toward gaining it. Two chapters on the virtue of studiousness aim to supply that vision, first in the example of a great orator and educator from the seventeenth century and then in an effort to delineate some ways in which the virtue might be profitably sought today.

The next five chapters present discussions of some of the tools of education. The first essay of this group shows how the first-hand experience of nature can shape and prepare our minds for the task of knowing. The second treats the human intellect's own special act, reasoning, through an examination of one of the most challenging books of Euclid's *Elements of Geometry*, a text widely held to be an ideal instrument for the training of the mind. The third and fourth chapters of this section shed light on the principal parts of humanistic formation, literary and historical studies, looking at them from the point of view of Aquinas's conception of the order of different fields of inquiry. The last of these tools is from the domain of natural science, an investigation of biology as it is being renewed today and becoming a more fitting component of a Catholic education than it has been in the century and a half since Darwin's *Origin of Species*.

The volume's final chapters are more synthetic and treat the school and the life of the educator as wholes within which to see these principles lived out and bearing fruit. The first is an attempt to give flesh to Blessed John Henry Newman's deepest convictions about education. Newman's *Idea of a University* is an immortal text and justly celebrated, but it is best understood when read in concert with his other writings on education and against the background of his life as an educator. The second is an interpretation of the philosophical life and labors of Alasdair MacIntyre, whose own writings on education are an indispensable resource today because of his uncanny ability to direct our attention to the questions we most need to ask. Indeed, MacIntyre's life-long reflection upon the tools and methods of education make him the ideal craftsman-educator of our time, and his ardent quest for wisdom has made him an admirable example of the Catholic tradition he has done so much to serve.

As a whole, this volume is offered to my fellow teachers with great esteem for their commitment to the common good of truth, and in homage to my own teachers, without whose efforts my steps along the path to wisdom would have been merely so many stumbles and falls. May we all find joy and consolation by laboring in imitation of Jesus Christ, the great teacher.

1

The Cultural Tragedy of the Enlightenment

PARTISANS AND CRITICS OF the Enlightenment alike acknowledge that mankind has in recent centuries turned away from the knowledge of God and toward the knowledge of man and of the material world. It belongs to the poet to ponder commonplaces such as this one and to express them with vigor and precision, in language that alerts us to the presence of deeper truths. A poet distinguished for his insight and for the pathos with which he expressed the plight of modern man was T. S. Eliot, who famously asked, "Where is the wisdom we have lost in knowledge?"[1] Already in the 1930s, Eliot had been able to perceive that modern man had lost the ability to be silent, had forgotten the proper signification of words, and, adrift upon a sea of information, had lost sight of his beginning and his end. He saw that the principles upon which the modern world had been founded were even then working themselves out to their necessary conclusion. We now know the end to which those principles have brought us, living as we do amidst the tragedy we have learned to call the culture of death.

---

1. T. S. Eliot, "Choruses from 'The Rock,'" in *Collected Poems, 1909–1962* (New York, 1970), 147.

In his great encyclical *Evangelium Vitae*, St. John Paul II explained that "in seeking the deepest roots of the struggle between the culture of life and the culture of death . . . we have to go to the heart of the tragedy being experienced by modern man: the eclipse of the sense of God and of man."[2] It is surprising to hear a Pope speak of the development of modern culture as a kind of tragedy. Do we not see all around us a culture in the full confidence of its mature development? Are we not experiencing reason's victory over prejudice, error, and the limitations of our nature? How could the modern world, with all of its technical ability and educational opportunity, be understood as tragic? Yet John Paul II insisted upon the word. The "end result" of the development of modern culture, he wrote, is "tragic," because "conscience itself, darkened as it were by . . . widespread conditioning, is finding it increasingly difficult to distinguish between good and evil." Could there be a more awful fate for man, created in the image of God, than to lose sight of the good? John Paul II spoke of this loss as having been abetted by a "conditioning" caused by our culture, in which "the values of being are replaced by those of having."[3] This culture of having is the creation of the Enlightenment. At the heart of the Enlightenment was a quest for material and bodily goods to be provided by the technological mastery of nature. This ideal, pursued relentlessly and with increasing devotion over the last three centuries, has created a culture characterized by the obscuring of the truth and the profusion of vain distractions. "Where is the wisdom we have lost in knowledge?" It is where it ever was, in the heart of the Church, in the ideal of Christian contemplation. If we would regain this wisdom, and begin to undo the errors and heal the damage of the culture of death, then we must first understand the nature and consequences of the Enlightenment ideal of knowledge.

---

2. John Paul II, *Evangelium Vitae*, #21, Vatican translation.

3. *Evangelium Vitae*, #s 3, 23.

The Enlightenment Ideal

It is more common to depict the Enlightenment as a movement of criticism than as a positive ideal. Thus Louis Dupré has described the Enlightenment as "first and foremost a breakthrough in critical consciousness."[4] The Enlightenment certainly did advocate loosening the ties of dogma and tradition. Even such a negative formulation, however, points to the positive ideal of rational autonomy, that is, self-rule by reason. Two works stand out for the clarity with which they expressed this ideal: the *Encyclopedia* of Denis Diderot and Jean d'Alembert, and Immanuel Kant's "What Is Enlightenment?" A consideration of these two celebrated works will allow us to hear the Enlightenment profess its ideal in its own words.

Diderot and d'Alembert have been overshadowed by their more famous contemporaries Voltaire and Rousseau, yet their contribution to the Enlightenment was equally influential. Their *Encyclopedia, or Reasoned Dictionary of the Sciences, the Arts, and the Trades*, was the period's monumental work and may be fittingly taken as the eighteenth-century rival to Aquinas's *Summa Theologiae*.[5] In his *Preliminary Discourse* to the *Encyclopedia*, d'Alembert as much as invited the comparison by pouring scorn upon his medieval ancestors in terms that were difficult to misunderstand. "The careful examination of Nature and the grand study of mankind," he asserted, "were [then] replaced by a thousand frivolous questions concerning abstract and metaphysical beings—questions whose solution, good or bad, often required much subtlety, and consequently a great abuse of the intelligence."[6] D'Alembert and Diderot understood their *Encyclopedia* to be laying the foundation for an edifice of learning that would transcend all prior efforts of synthesis.

---

4. Louis Dupré, *The Enlightenment and the Intellectual Foundations of Modern Culture* (New Haven: Yale University Press, 2004), xiii.

5. See Alasdair MacIntyre, *Three Rival Versions of Moral Enquiry: Encyclopedia, Genealogy, and Tradition* (Notre Dame: University of Notre Dame Press, 1988).

6. Jean d'Alembert, *Preliminary Discourse to the Encyclopedia of Diderot*, trans. Richard N. Schwab (Chicago: University of Chicago, 1995), 62.

The most evident difference between the *Encyclopedia* and Aquinas's *Summa* is that the former is arranged alphabetically, whereas the latter followed an order of exposition dictated by the science of sacred doctrine. Aquinas began with God, passed to the Creation, and within it, to man, and then treated the return of the Creation to God through man's redemption in Christ. The *Encyclopedia* followed no such order, for its concern was different. It included entries on religious subjects, but it also included articles on the arts and trades, from military fortifications to animal husbandry. To organize such a collection according to the "order of ideas," Diderot argued, would have made it "less convenient for most of our readers."[7]

In spite of its pragmatic organization, the *Encyclopedia* was animated by a certain conception of the unity of knowledge, a conception defended by d'Alembert in a lengthy *Preliminary Discourse* to the *Encyclopedia's* first volume, published in 1751. D'Alembert's *Discourse* began with an historical narrative of the origin of human learning sharply at odds with the theory given by Aristotle and accepted by Aquinas. Unlike Aristotle, who attested to man's natural desire to know and associated that desire with a kind of wonder about the order of the universe as a whole, d'Alembert thought human investigations to proceed primarily from the body's need to be protected against external causes of pain. It followed that the ultimate test of knowledge was in its usefulness in contributing to what he called the "sovereign good of the present life ... the exemption from pain." The body's potential needs, however, are "endlessly multiplying." Accordingly, the *Encyclopedia* would be a lengthy document, written by "scholars well-versed in the particular discipline which was to be their share of the work," and including eleven large volumes of high-quality engravings of buildings, tools, and machines to accompany its seventeen volumes of text.[8]

---

7. Diderot's prospectus was incorporated into the third part of d'Alembert's *Preliminary Discourse*. Schwab, ed., 113.

8. D'Alembert, 10, 14, and 112. For the history of the *Encyclopedia*, see Schwab's "Introduction" to his edition of the *Preliminary Discourse* and Raymond Birn, "Encyclopédie," in Alan Charles Kors, et al., eds. *Encyclopedia of the Enlightenment*, 4 volumes (New York, 2003), I:403–9.

Its genesis in the work of experts is the most important characteristic of the *Encyclopedia*. Each of the various arts or trades contains enough particular knowledge to fill up more than a lifetime of studies. If the work were to be a monument to a "philosophical century," it would have to be written by specialists.[9] The task of the editors was to suggest the connections among the various articles written by the team of experts, which they did in three ways: through a system of cross-referencing, by the provision of a schema or tree of knowledge, and in the text of d'Alembert's *Preliminary Discourse*. Yet the knowledge of the connections among the various entries, d'Alembert warned, was not to be thought supremely valuable: "a single reasoned article on a particular object of science or art includes more material substance than all the possible divisions and subdivisions of the general terms."[10] No "two persons could treat all the science and the arts," nor could any two persons, let alone one, judge the *Encyclopedia* as a whole: only "scholars," with an emphasis on the plural, would be capable of that task.[11] Aristotle's ideal of *paideia*, which may be translated as "liberal education," was thus set aside in favor of a new ideal of specialized expertise, because the kind of knowledge that was being sought, useful knowledge, demanded the change.

Aquinas's *Summa*, the work of one wise man, was a labor of reflection. Aquinas's tools were those of Aristotelian logic; his materials were, on the one hand, our common experience of the world, and, on the other, Holy Scripture as interpreted by the Fathers of the Church. The *Encyclopedia*, however, would seek knowledge from other sources. "The single true method of philosophizing as physical scientists," wrote d'Alembert," consists either in the application of mathematical analysis to experiments, or in observation alone."[12] Observation and experiments, multiplied many times, by teams of researchers over

---

9. Diderot, "Encyclopedia," in Peter Gay, ed., *The Enlightenment: A Comprehensive Anthology* (New York, 1973), 288.

10. D'Alembert, 58.

11. Ibid., 3.

12. Ibid., 25.

many years and with a reliable source of funding: this was the plan laid down by Descartes and Bacon early in the seventeenth century and gradually put into practice through the creation of academies and philosophical societies dedicated to experiments. The scholastic reliance upon the authority of ancient texts had proven to be stultifying. Had not Aristotle and Ptolemy erred in their claims about the heavens? Archimedes, therefore, was to be preferred to Aristotle, and artisans rather than scholars were to provide "the most admirable evidences of the sagacity, the patience, and the resources of the mind."[13] On this point, d'Alembert's thinking was rigidly consistent: the measure of true learning was henceforth to be the unbiased testimony of the senses, and, therefore, "young men" were held to be "perhaps the best judges in philosophical and many other matters."[14]

Experiments and observation most reliably and immediately provide knowledge of things that can be sensed. Accordingly, the *Encyclopedia* differed from Aquinas's *Summa* both in its conception of the end of knowledge and in the type or quality of knowledge that was to be sought. For Aquinas, the purpose of knowledge was to help man to attain his ultimate end: the vision of the Blessed Trinity. The knowledge of spiritual realities, and supremely the knowledge of God, was to be preferred to all other kinds of knowledge. The *Encyclopedia* embraced a more earthly goal. Diderot spoke of the "happiness of future ages and that of the entire human race," to be gained through a knowledge of the physical causes of things.[15] These causes, however, were not so much plumbed in themselves as they were examined in their effects, which might be harnessed to man's physical needs. Motion, therefore, the analysis of which had been the chief concern of Aristotle's *Physics* and the basis of Aquinas's first proof of the existence of God, was declared to be "an enigma" by d'Alembert.[16] To know the natures of things was less important to him than to be able to master their effects:

---

13. Ibid., 42. On Archimedes, see d'Alembert, 58.
14. Ibid., 90.
15. Diderot, in *The Enlightenment: A Comprehensive Anthology*, 290.
16. D'Alembert, 27.

"The mere fact that we have occasionally found concrete advantages in certain fragments of knowledge, when they were hitherto unsuspected, authorizes us to regard all investigations begun out of pure curiosity as being potentially useful to us."[17]

What seems finally to have been envisioned by the editors of the *Encyclopedia* is a science that will, as d'Alembert put it, bring about "exemption from pain."[18] That science will allow not only the mastery of inanimate nature, but also of man himself. It will be a social science, a science to govern morals, the economy, jurisprudence, and politics. This is the vision that informed the contribution to the *Encyclopedia* of Anne-Robert-Jacques Turgot, the entry for "Foundation." The essay treated endowments, such as might support a charitable work like an orphanage, and argued that the intentions of the donor should always give way to the needs of the present generation. Turgot's essay seemed merely to be a plea for prudence, but his argument actually reposed upon a new conception of reason: the prudence of the ruler and the wisdom of the ages would bow to what he called the "political sciences."[19] This desire to create a science of society was at the heart of the Enlightenment. What the philosophers of the age sought was a social science that would be a science in the modern sense of the term. Their ideal was neatly expressed by Condorcet, a disciple of both d'Alembert and Turgot, as well as a contributor to the *Encyclopedia*, in his 1782 speech to the French Academy: "In meditating on the nature of the moral sciences, one cannot indeed help seeing that, based like the physical sciences upon the observation of facts, they must follow the same methods, acquire an equally exact and precise language, attain the same degree of certainty."[20]

---

17. Ibid., 16.

18. Ibid., 10.

19 Turgot, "Foundation," in Keith Baker, ed., *The Old Regime and the French Revolution* (Chicago: University of Chicago Press, 1987), 91.

20 Condorcet, "Reception Speech at the French Academy," in Keith Michael Baker, ed., *Condorcet: Selected Writings* (Indianapolis: Bobbs Merrill, 1976), 6. On Condorcet's debts to Diderot and d'Alembert, see Baker, *Condorcet: From Natural Phi-*

Condorcet's hope for the discovery of a new moral science was matched by the optimism of his German contemporary, Immanuel Kant, whose essay "What Is Enlightenment?" is arguably the movement's quintessential work. The essay began with a memorable definition: Enlightenment is "mankind's exit from its self-incurred immaturity."[21] The explanation that ensued was an uncompromising statement of the ideal of rational autonomy. What stood in the way of rational autonomy was, in the first place, "laziness and cowardice." "If I have a book that has understanding for me, a pastor who has a conscience for me, a doctor who judges my diet for me, and so forth, surely I do not need to trouble myself." Yet there were other obstacles than laziness, and the worst was the authority of pastors: "Those guardians, who have graciously taken up the oversight of mankind, take care that the far greater part of mankind regard the step to maturity as not only difficult but also very dangerous." Kant proceeded with a biting metaphor: "After they have first made their domestic animals stupid and carefully prevented these placid creatures from daring to take even one step out of the leading strings of the cart to which they are tethered, they show them the danger that threatens them if they attempt to proceed on their own." Kant's ultimate foe was religious authority. Should a religious community bind itself to an unchanging creed, it would commit what he called a "crime against human nature," because to do so would be to stand against the "progress" that is human nature's "original destiny." Immaturity in "religious matters," moreover, he thought to be "the most harmful as well as the most dishonorable kind of immaturity,"[22] because the good of humanity, in the last analysis, consists in the realization of "the inclination and the vocation for free thinking" that exists in man according to his nature.

---

losophy to Social Mathematics (Chicago: University of Chicago Press, 1975), 1-82.

21. Kant, "An Answer to the Question: What Is Enlightenment?", trans. James Schmidt, in Schmidt, ed., *What Is Enlightenment? Eighteenth-Century Answers and Twentieth-Century Questions* (Berkeley: University of California Press, 1996), 58.

22. Kant, in Schmidt, ed., 58–59, 61, 63.

Kant's conception of the good for man consisting in rational autonomy came with a social corollary: the freedom of the individual to use his reason to contribute to the Enlightenment of the human race. Kant's essay, in fact, is a brief for what a later age might call freedom of expression: "For this enlightenment . . . nothing more is required than freedom; and indeed the most harmless form of all things that may be called freedom: namely, the freedom to make a public use of one's reason in all matters."[23] All European countries in the eighteenth century had some form of censorship exercised in the name of confessional uniformity and for the preservation of public morals. This censorship resulted in inconveniences for the leading protagonists of the Enlightenment, such as the necessity to have their works published in the Dutch republic and smuggled across European borders, or even the occasional flight from the law or trip to the Bastille. Kant's concern, however, was the principle rather than the details of the practice of free expression. Thus he praised Frederick II of Prussia for having "freed mankind from immaturity and left them free to use their own reason in everything that is a matter of conscience," in spite of the fact that he had retained political censorship. This last form of censorship would, however, pass away in time, when the people "become more and more capable of acting freely," and the government finds it "to its advantage to treat man . . . in accord with his dignity."[24] Kant's conception of the free use of reason, joined with the *Encyclopedia*'s program for the mastery of nature through the progress of experimental science, together form the fundamental pillars of modern culture. Freedom and science are now our highest shared ideals. We may ask to what end we have been brought by following them so intently.

---

23. Kant, in Schmidt, ed., 59.

24. Ibid., 62, 63. On censorship, see Jonathan I. Israel, *Radical Enlightenment: Philosophy and the Making of Modernity, 1650–1750* (New York: Oxford University Press, 2001), 97–118. On the significance of Kant's argument about the press, see Roger Chartier, *The Cultural Origins of the French Revolution*, tr. Lydia G. Cochrane (Durham, NC: Duke University Press, 1991), 23–27.

Consequences of the Enlightenment Ideal

In each of the leading features of the Enlightenment ideal of self-rule by reason we may perceive a tragic turning away of the mind from its Creator.

Let us return to the *Encyclopedia*. By setting the example of an alphabetical arrangement of articles written by a team of experts, the *Encyclopedia* has helped to shape modern intellectual and cultural development. Our culture, academic and otherwise, is one of experts, whose attainments within their chosen fields are difficult if not pointless to contest. What we have lost is a shared culture of the search for the highest truths. To us, all truths are equal; their only order is alphabetical. All of our experts, accordingly, are in some sense equal. They each have authority in their discipline and none outside it. And as really very few of our scholars or cultural figures are specialists in the highest truths—the truths traditionally contemplated by metaphysicians and theologians—we have created a culture in which the vast majority of the brightest and most highly educated specialize in subjects that are merely useful. This trend is as strong in the humanities as in the sciences, for the humanities long ago took the sciences for their model. The overwhelming tendency in modern education throughout the Western world is toward early specialization in fields that the Christian intellectual tradition has generally seen as being of subordinate value. Our educational practice, then, leads men and women away from the pursuit of wisdom.

The second leading characteristic of the *Encyclopedia* was its emphasis on empirical knowledge, especially as derived from experiments. From these empirical studies we have reaped immeasurable dividends. Yet the culture of experimentation has always been associated with a Promethean cast of mind. Descartes, for one, dared to hope that by progress in the study of medicine "we might free ourselves from innumerable diseases . . . and perhaps even from the infirmities of old age."[25] Francis Bacon's visionary *New Atlantis* presented a

---

25. Descartes, *Discourse on Method*, trans. John Cottingham, et alia, in *Philosophical Writings of Descartes* (Cambridge: Cambridge University Press, 1985), 143.

world in which man would no longer need to conquer his passions in order to gain the benefits of temperance: his experiments would yield him foods and medicines capable of guaranteeing health, beauty, and strength. The culture of experimentation was from the first impatient of the suggestion that experimental practices might be morally ambiguous. Thus Voltaire punctuated his call for widespread inoculation for smallpox with the acerbic jab, "if the clergy and the physicians will but give them leave to do it."[26] In our day, the transgressive potential of unbridled experimentation is well known, with examples ranging from the abuse of steroids by athletes to the horrifying call for the experimental study of stem cells harvested from the bodies of children murdered in their mothers' wombs or organs harvested from human clones. Like Victor Frankenstein or the astrologers of yore, we are insatiable in our quest for knowledge and are being led to seek it in sources from which little good can be expected.

Our thirst for useful knowledge has long been joined to a comparative lack of interest in the transcendent. D'Alembert followed Descartes in presenting the essential knowledge of the souls and of God as easy to come by, quickly mastered, and, finally, of little moment.[27] The enduring irony of the Enlightenment is that its quest for knowledge has been joined to a skepticism about the spiritual realm, and even at times its dogmatic rejection. There is nothing intrinsic to experimental or artistic knowledge that causes its possessor to reject God. The problem lies in the seeking of it. For a man need not be a metaphysician in order to attain the kind of knowledge that promises mastery of nature, and so when his desire for useful knowledge overmasters him, he willingly sets aside what he does not value. The consequent habit of seeking first and above all else the knowledge of physical realities—a habit that has shaped our common culture—in the end draws one imperceptibly away from the world of the spirit. Even modern agnostics

---

26. Voltaire, *Letters Concerning the English Nation*, ed. Nicholas Cronk (Oxford: Oxford University Press, 1994), 48.

27. D'Alembert, 12-14; may be compared to Descartes's *Discourse on Method*, parts 1 and 4.

have affirmed this tendency, and most hauntingly Charles Darwin, who confessed the "curious and lamentable loss" of his sensitivity to beauty: "My mind seems to have become a kind of machine for grinding general laws out of large collections of facts."[28] Bacon, Voltaire, d'Alembert, and countless other Enlightenment thinkers idolized the inventor, without realizing that the contemplative monk whose life they saw as useless was in possession of truths higher and more indispensable for human happiness than the ones they so eagerly sought.

Then finally there is the Enlightenment's quest for a science of man, a project of such hubris that it seems at times to be a re-enactment of man's first sin. Adam and Eve did not want to be ruled by God or to rely upon his Providence to dispose future events for their good. They wanted to rule themselves, and sought by eating the forbidden fruit to gain the kind of knowledge that would enable them to master future contingent events.[29] As unpredictable as are tropical storms and earthquakes, these disasters pale before the complexity and unpredictability of the human will. A science that would allow man's choices to be known before they are made is, in effect, what Enlightenment social science has sought to be. The more determined theorists have attempted to make their science perfect by denying the freedom of the will. The social engineering that has resulted from such systems shows that the quest for a social science has led mankind into deeper errors. From the deportation of the retrograde to the Gulag to the forced sterilization of the so-called unfit in the laboratories of the eugenicists, the twentieth century saw sufficient horrors to discredit social science forever. Yet old ideals are slow in dying, and the Enlightenment belief in the perfectibility of man remains strong.

---

28. *The Autobiography of Charles Darwin*, ed. Nora Barlow (New York: Norton, 1958), 139.

29. See *Summa Theologiae* II-II, 163, 2 and Alasdair MacIntyre, *After Virtue: A Study in Moral Theory*, 3rd edition (1981; Notre Dame: University of Notre Dame Press, 2007), 96–97: "It is precisely insofar as we differ from God that unpredictability invades our lives. This way of putting the point has one particular merit: it suggests precisely what project those who seek to eliminate unpredictability from the social world or to deny it may in fact be engaging in."

Christians may soon be the only people on the planet who will wish to give birth to children with genetic defects. How long will we be allowed to do so?

The cultural consequences of the Enlightenment ideal as defined by Kant's "What Is Enlightenment?" are, if possible, even more dire. For with Kant, the error is not that knowledge is being sought immoderately or by illicit means, but that the end for which the knowledge is sought is itself problematic. In the first place there is Kant's ideal of rational autonomy. The individual man or woman is to rule him- or herself by reason alone, without reference to inherited conceptions or religious creeds. At the heart of the search for knowledge, as Kant understood it, was the criticism of authority, and above all religious authority. Knowledge-claims that are made use of for the sake of emancipating through criticism are, in effect, being used to proclaim the self-sufficiency of the individual. With Kant we see that the Enlightenment criticism of authority is not innocent; it engendered a rebellious habit of mind. From the eighteenth century to the twenty-first, rebellion has been the leading trait of Western, and now world-wide political and cultural change. From the French Revolution to the Sexual Revolution, the characteristic hymn of the modern world is the Tempter's "I will not serve," often set to music that stirs the passions. "Knowledge puffs up," warned St. Paul (1 Cor. 8:1), especially the knowledge sought by the Enlightenment.

Kant's second goal in writing "What is Enlightenment?" was to vindicate the freedom of the public use of reason, and, on that count, he long ago carried the day. Yet the untrammeled freedom of expression that now holds sway is not without its negative consequences. The first is that with the demise of censorship throughout most of the Western world, we are now free to seek what passes for knowledge in order to use it to commit sins, and sins most base and demeaning indeed. At the heart of the Enlightenment quest for free expression and freedom of the press was moral license. Kant himself seems to have been innocent of this failing. Yet many were not. Diderot, for instance, wrote works that can only be described as pornographic, and he was not alone, as is well known from Robert Darnton's documentation of what he called the "forbidden best-sellers of pre-Revolutionary France."[30] In our own day, the champions of civil liberty are all too often those who derive vast profits from pornography and other forms of cultural and psychological exploitation.

A second consequence of free expression, less distressing than the first but perhaps as great an obstacle to the culture of life, is the fragmentation of our culture into a welter of vain distractions. It is probably too soon to tell what will be the lasting cultural significance of the internet, but we can at least say that it seems to be creating a world in which the individual may be said to choose his own culture. Some Christians have celebrated the diffusion of the alternative cultural spaces the internet provides as a means of subverting the dominance of the secularist media. Who indeed would shed a tear for the decline in market share of the major media networks or newspapers? Yet for every Christian website there are many others that are far from Christian. The logic of the internet is a logic of individual choice. By exercising their choice, individuals are retreating further and further into their chosen sub-cultures and micro-communities, and, as the line between providers and consumers of content continues to blur, and as personal web pages multiply to infinity, the internet is more and more clearly a cavernous room filled with millions of people shouting to make themselves heard. Are the few voices that really matter able to make themselves heard amidst the din of these thousands of insistent soliloquies? The deep problem with the kind of cultural fragmentation that we are seeking is that it militates against the universality of the Christian faith. There is a legitimate diversity of forms of Christian life—there are many gardens in the Church and many rooms in the heavenly mansion—but the Faith does have its own culture, indeed the only true culture because the only one founded upon the right worship of God. Christians cannot worship the contemporary idol named diversity. Nor

---

30. On Diderot's *Les Bijoux Indiscrets* (1748), see Arthur M. Wilson, *Diderot* (New York, 1972), 83–87. On the role of pornography in the Enlightenment, see Robert Darnton, *The Forbidden Best-Sellers of Pre-Revolutionary France* (New York, 1996), and Israel, *Radical Enlightenment*, 91–96.

can we rest content in a culture, if it can be called a culture at all, characterized by myriad choices presented in a bewildering array of media.

On balance, then, the Enlightenment ideal of useful knowledge gained through experimentation and promulgated to freely choosing individuals has ushered in a culture characterized by the darkening of the mind and the distraction of the senses, that is, by the vice of curiosity.[31] Enlightenment culture is a culture of curiosity. It is a sign of the Enlightenment's temporary victory that our age no longer even considers curiosity to be the name of a vice. In our common culture of media consumerism we are more likely to hear celebrations of diversity and choice than we are warnings about our over-saturation with content. Nor can we expect much help from the academy, because universities seem to be perpetually creating new disciplines, centers, and programs, while scholars prosecute their studies with the same kind of industrialized productivity that characterizes the popular media.[32] The remedy to our culture of curiosity is found in the Church's call that we contemplate the face of God, as St. John Paul II urged in *Novo Millennio Ineunte*. Contemplation is our destiny in heaven; it is our highest calling here on earth. To acquiesce in the Enlightenment's culture of curiosity is to trade in our birthright for a bowl of lentils. It is not a bargain we should make willingly.

A Return to Wisdom

In the *Pastoral Constitution on the Church in the Modern World*, the fathers of the Second Vatican Council warned our parents' generation about its uncritical enthusiasm for modern science and technology and reaffirmed the priority of wisdom. The Council's admonition is inspiring, if also sobering:

---

31. See *Summa Theologiae* II-II, 167, 1.

32. For a similar assessment of the modern academy, see Paul J. Griffiths, *Religious Reading: The Place of Reading in the Practice of Religion* (New York, 1999), esp. 40–54 and 182–88.

> The intellectual nature of the human person is perfected by
> wisdom and needs to be. For wisdom gently attracts the mind
> of man to a quest and a love for what is true and good. Steeped
> in wisdom, man passes through visible realities to those which
> are unseen. Our era needs such wisdom more than bygone ages
> if the discoveries made by man are to be further humanized.
> For the future of the world stands in peril unless wiser men are
> forthcoming.[33]

Living as we do amidst the horror of the culture of death, we
know that our generation must provide men and women of deep and
abiding wisdom if we are to avoid destroying our own human nature.

Our task, then, is to repair the cultural tragedy of the Enlightenment. Only a fool would be undaunted when faced by such a challenge. The obstacles before us seem almost insurmountable. Leaving
aside those posed by the world, we see in our own minds and souls the
wounds of the Enlightenment. We are all specialists now, and we live
and work in a world that demands specialized competence from us,
competence won at great cost over many years of study and experience. We are all consumers of the manifold forms of media that sur-
round us in our every waking moment. By the time we have reached
maturity, our intellectual habits have been formed, and our habits are
those of the Enlightenment.

Our first task then, prior to working for broader cultural renewal,
is to admit that the characteristic faults of our age are faults from
which we personally suffer. In this admission, we follow the example
of St. Augustine. In the tenth book of his *Confessions*, St. Augustine
presented to God the vicious tendencies of his own soul and asked
Christ to heal him and to effect his continuing conversion. Having
treated each of his five senses as sources of temptation, he proceeded
to discuss a "different kind of temptation, more dangerous than these
because it is more complicated," the mind's "propensity to use the
sense of the body, not for self-indulgence of a physical kind, but for
the satisfaction of its own inquisitiveness." St. Augustine mourned his

---

33. *The Documents of Vatican II*, ed. Walter M. Abbott, S.J. (New York, 1966), 213.

inclination when traveling through the countryside to watch a dog chase a hare and thus to allow himself to be distracted from "whatever serious thoughts occupied [his] mind." We might find this example far removed from our own experience, especially in light of the much graver source of distraction that is the internet. Yet the principle adduced by St. Augustine is a perennial one. "My life is full of such faults," he wrote, "and my only hope is in your boundless mercy. For when our hearts become repositories piled high with such worthless stock as this, it is the cause of interruption and distraction from our prayers."[34] St. Augustine would teach us that an immoderate and disordered desire for knowledge frustrates our ability to be attentive to the source of all knowledge.

"Be still," says the Lord, "and know that I am God" (Ps. 46:10). His injunction concerns more than our limbs, it concerns our senses and our desires, and our desire for knowledge. St. John Paul II challenged us to have "the courage to adopt a new lifestyle, consisting in making practical choices . . . on the basis of a correct scale of values: the primacy of being over having, of the person over things."[35] By embracing a kind of asceticism with respect to the media and bridling our desire for knowledge, and by rededicating ourselves to the ordered search for and consideration of the highest truths, we will begin to heal our own souls, and, later, perhaps much later, find that we have become more effective in transmitting that "sense of God and of man" which alone can undo the cultural tragedy of the Enlightenment.

---

34. Augustine, *Confessions*, X.35, trans. R. S. Pine-Coffin (London: Penguin, 1961), 241, 243–44.

35. *Evangelium Vitae*, #98.

2

A Model of Studiousness

"LET ME TELL YOU, my God, how I squandered the brains you gave me on foolish delusions."[1] St. Augustine knew from bitter experience that if man's desire to know is to serve him, it must be bridled by the will and ruled by reason, must be subject, that is, to the virtue of studiousness.[2] It is a virtue that, being foreign to our temper, is difficult for us to understand. For in the long years since Eliot mourned the passing of the "wisdom we have lost in knowledge," we have so immoderately partaken of encyclopedic learning that we are likely to have a habit that inclines more toward curiosity than to studiousness. If we seek to recover the ideal of studiousness, the true mean with respect to the desire to know, we would therefore do well to turn to the witness of the tradition. One model of this virtue comes to us from the age of Louis XIV in the person of the great orator, Jacques-Bénigne Bossuet.

In his day, Bossuet (1627–1704) was recognized as one of the most learned churchmen in Europe. Today he is little known outside of Francophone lands, which is lamentable, if for no other reason than

---

1. St. Augustine, *Confessions*, I.17, trans. R. S. Pine-Coffin (London: Penguin, 1961), 37.
2. See, for instance, St. Augustine, *On the Profit of Believing* §22, trans. C. L. Cornish, in *Basic Writings of St. Augustine*, ed. Whitney J. Oates, 2 volumes (New York: Random House, 1948), I: 414.

that it indicates the loss of the riches of his oratory. For its sonorous tone, for the beauty of its order, and for its penetrating vision into the depths of the soul, Bossuet's oratory endures as one of the highest achievements of the Catholic Baroque. And his erudition was by no means exhausted in rhetorical composition. As the tutor to the Dauphin in the 1670s and Bishop of Meaux and royal advisor until his death in 1704, he was called upon to write a wide variety of pedagogical, pastoral, and learned works, from letters of spiritual direction, to textbooks, to apologetic works of tremendous weight such as his *Exposition of Catholic Doctrine* (1671) and the *History of the Variations of the Protestant Churches* (1688). By the last decade of his life, when he was exchanging letters with Leibniz about the prospects of the reunion of the Protestants with the Catholic Church, Bossuet had become an honored voice of the living Catholic tradition: to the faithful, a champion, and to the nascent Enlightenment, a barrier to be overcome or cast aside.[3]

There are two reasons why Bossuet can serve as a compelling model of studiousness. The first is that he defended and practiced the virtue at a time when it was being rejected by the new learning of the Renaissance. The virtues are not necessarily the stronger for being opposed, but when they are opposed, those who would uphold them are forced to reflect upon them as ideals with a sharpened awareness. The second reason is that he pursued wisdom within the context of an active life. From his early days as a Doctor of the Sorbonne until his death, his life of study and writing was always at the service of the pressing needs of the Church and of his roles as educator and pastor. In our day, similarly, most of those who pursue wisdom within the Catholic intellectual tradition do so not in the cloister, but in the academy, whose groves are not so well-suited to contemplative repose. And so, while Bossuet himself would tell us that if we wish to be studious we should imitate St. Bernard, St. Gregory, and St. Augustine,

---

3. See the classic characterization of Bossuet in Paul Hazard, *The European Mind, 1680–1715*, trans. J. Lewis May (Cleveland: World Publishing Co., 1963), 198–236.

we may gain from him some insights more immediately applicable to our condition than from those who were more deeply rooted in the liturgical life and religious community.

Curiosity Becomes an Ideal

The full meaning of the virtue of studiousness is difficult to appreciate without reference to the opposing vice of curiosity. In his discussion of the vice of curiosity, Aquinas points to four ways in which the natural desire for knowledge can be wrongly directed. The third of these will be our chief concern because it came to typify the new learning of the Renaissance: "when man desires to know the truth about creatures, without referring it to its due end, which is the knowledge of God."[4] It would be difficult to imagine a more complete embodiment of the vice than the new learning of the seventeenth century. Consider Descartes's prohibition of the search for final causes, or, more provocatively, the name Bacon gave to his imaginary academy, the College of the Six Days Works, a name suggesting that productive work and not contemplation was man's highest good.[5] For their audacity in proposing principles starkly contrary to those of the Aristotelian tradition, Bacon and Descartes have long been numbered among its chief rivals. Principles, however, rarely spring to life fully formed. They more often grow slowly in a soil prepared by gradual changes in practice. Around Bacon and Descartes stood an array of men-of-letters, philologists, antiquarians, experimental philosophers, and autodidacts, in a word, the curious. In the lives and works of these many inquirers the principles expressed by the more well-known thinkers found their origin and their elaboration.

Two texts from the late Renaissance reveal the inordinate desire for knowledge that characterized the new learning: Gabriel Naudé's

---

4. *Summa Theologiae* II-II, Q. 167, Art. 1. Translations from the *Summa Theologiae* are my own, unless otherwise noted.
5. See Descartes, *Meditation #4* and *Principles of Philosophy* I.28; Bacon, *New Atlantis*, in *Francis Bacon: The Major Works*, ed. Brian Vickers (New York: Oxford University Press, 2002), 471.

Advis pour dresser une Bibliothèque (1627) and Pierre Gassendi's *Life of Peiresc* (1641). Naudé, a librarian, and Gassendi, a cleric and philosopher, were both members of the emerging Republic of Letters; their works shed light upon the mentality of those who prepared the ground for and welcomed the innovations of Bacon and Descartes. In these two treatises can be seen three common characteristics of the new learning: first, that the word curiosity had become the name of a positive character trait and even of an ideal; second, that the ideal consisted in the lack of restraint in the pursuit of knowledge; third, that new institutions were emerging to support and instantiate the new ideal.

Naudé's *Advice for Fitting Out a Library* was a courtly work, addressed by a savant to his patron, who was a member of the legal aristocracy bitten by the love of books. Written with all the fervor of youthful conviction, Naudé's essay proposed a refinement of the Renaissance cultural ideal: the learned courtier's books were not to be beautifully bound, artfully arranged, or magnificently housed, but useful, up-to-date, and numerous. In his *Advice* the forms of the word curious appeared regularly, most often when qualifying a book as curious, which served chiefly to indicate its rarity, but sometimes when directly referring to a scholar's desire for knowledge. In those cases the term was not used with a negative meaning; one commentator has observed that Naudé used *curieux* as a synonym for *docte* (learned).[6] Gassendi's *Life of Peiresc* was written less from a desire to please a patron than from admiration for a celebrated member of the Republic of Letters whom Gassendi commended as a model for his "unquenchable thirst after knowledge" and his "unwearied care to advance all ingenious and liberal arts." Here, too, the word curious was employed as a term of approbation, as when Gassendi said of the young Peiresc that "his most curious mind began to burn like fire in a wood."[7] For both

---

6. Paul Nelles, "The Library as an Instrument of Discovery: Gabriel Naudé and the Uses of History," in Donald R. Kelley, ed., *History and the Disciplines: The Reclassification of Knowledge in Early Modern Europe* (Rochester, NY: University of Rochester Press, 1997), 44.

7. Gassendi, *The Mirrour of True Nobility and Gentility: Being the Life of the renowned*

Gassendi and Naudé, giving the word curious a neutral or even positive connotation accorded with their broader doctrine. Both scholars shared the conviction that the pursuit of knowledge should suffer no restraint.

The emerging Renaissance ideal of curiosity was the precise opposite of Aquinas's conception of studiousness. For Aquinas, studiousness owed its name to its secondary quality of removing the obstacles to learning posed by man's distaste for the pains of study (*labores inquirendi*), but its essential function was to curb the desire for knowledge. "Studiousness," he said, with his usual economy, "consists in restraint."[8] But the new learning was departing from the older, theological model of learning by seeking a different kind of universality. Thus Gassendi lauded Peiresc in these terms: "Being moderate in all other things, he seemed only immoderate in his desire of knowledge; and never man was more desirous than he, to run through the famous encyclopedia, or whole circle of the arts."[9] Naudé made the lack of restraint in the pursuit of knowledge almost the measure of human happiness. "If it is possible to have in this world some sovereign good, some perfect and complete felicity," then, he explained, it was to be found in a library of a learned man who "does not desire books so that they might be the ornament of his dining room so much as the instruments of his studies." With the right library, a man "might know all things, see all things, be ignorant of nothing;" he would be "the absolute master of this contentment, that he might arrange it according to his fantasies, enjoy it when he will, leave it when it please him, and, without suffering contradiction, without labor, and without pain he may instruct

---

Nicolaus Claudius Fabricius, Lord of Peiresk, translated by W. Rand in 1657, ed. Oliver Thill (Haverford, PA: Infinity Publishing, 2003), 11, 22.

8. *Summa Theologiae* II-II, Q. 166, Art. 2, ad 3.

9. Gassendi, *Mirrour*, ed. Thill, 280. I respectfully differ from the judgment of Lynn Joy, who sees "mixed admiration and regret" in this and similar passages in which Gassendi "reluctantly acknowledged" Pieresc's immoderate desire for knowledge. See Lynn Sumida Joy, *Gassendi the Atomist: Advocate of History in an Age of Science* (Cambridge: Cambridge University Press, 1987), 59.

himself and know the most precise particulars."[10] To the partisans of the new learning, curiosity, the unchecked desire for knowledge, had become the name of a virtue. The desire for knowledge was a measure and rule unto itself.

To divine what was the end of the knowledge so eagerly sought by Naudé and Peiresc is not so simple a matter. Both acknowledged the duty to use the truth to convert heretics, yet their thoughts were clearly elsewhere. Naudé gives us a clue in his judgment that collections of ancient sources are most valuable for a library because of "the brevity of our life and the multitude of things that one must know today in order to be placed in the ranks of learned men." The library was also to have works by scholars of the present century, so that one could avoid being a pedant, that is, one who "disdains all the modern authors so that he might pay court only to a few of the ancients."[11] To be a member of good standing in the Republic of Letters was Naudé's goal. On a similar note, Gassendi painted the copious learning of Peiresc as being its own justification. In his *Life*, after a bewildering chronicle of his friend's interests, from the bones of saints to new stars, turtles to tulips, and Coptic manuscripts to Roman coins, he reported a conversation in which Peiresc had defended his antiquarian researches as worthy of praise because "they give light to the understanding of good authors," assist in knowing "the circumstances of histories," and cause "persons, things, and actions" to be "more deeply fixed in the mind."[12] One studies, then, in order to study with more understanding. Undergirding this reflexive justification is the unspoken premise that the best knowledge is that which is most recently acquired. Naudé's concern to have the latest texts by the most current scholars was matched by Peiresc's searching of the Mediterranean world for rare manuscripts, old in themselves, but new to the learned. If the merits of a bit of knowledge cannot be judged with respect to the object

---

10. Naudé, *Advis pour dresser une bibliothèque*, edition of 1644 (Paris: Isidore Lisieux, 1876), 12–13.

11. Naudé, *Advis*, 43 and 47.

12. Gassendi, *Mirrour*, ed. Thill, 292.

of the knowledge or the transformation that the knowledge effects in the knower, what remains is some quality that the knowledge brings with it, such as pleasure, usefulness, or fame, all of which are readily found in novelty. The most telling evidence that it was the love of the new that motivated Peiresc's studies is that Gassendi told the story of his discoveries and experiences in chronological order, with one thing simply following another in time. There was no single great achievement or guiding inquiry for him, he simply studied the old in order to find the new.

Institutions and practices soon came to embody this love of novelty. Naudé's *Advice* was the blueprint for just such an institution, a new kind of library, whose end was not the fame of the patron but "public use," and especially by the "least of men."[13] Wide use by many scholars being its end, the library's collection was to be arranged so as to be most easily accessible. For Naudé, this meant that the order of the books was not a matter of principle but of practice. He was content to maintain the established custom of separating volumes according to the various faculties of the university, but as the basis for the organization was now merely custom, "the traditional order of the disciplines" was placed "in a much weaker position."[14] Gassendi was less interested in the library than in the scholar who inhabited it. Peiresc had been more valuable than any collection of books; indeed, from Gassendi's portrait one might conclude that he had been essentially a reference librarian. For Peiresc had been prompt in the service of the Republic of Letters: "[H]e never stood considering, when occasion was offered to advance learning, and assist learned men." The books themselves were merely tools; the inquirer was the maker. Accordingly, Peiresc spent more time in his later years acquiring rare books and manuscripts for his correspondents than he did in reading them himself.[15] He stood at the heart of a vast correspondence network linking scholars from Alexandria to London, from Antwerp to Rome. Letter writ-

---

13. Naudé, *Advis*, 103.
14. Nelles, "The Library as an Instrument of Discovery," 46.
15. Gassendi, *Mirrour*, ed. Thill, 281, 288.

ing, the exchange of books, and conversations in libraries and salons: as the century wore on, these institutions grew and multiplied, to be joined by learned journals, academies of science, and, finally, coffee houses, all of them providing what one well-known journal of the day called "News from the Republic of Letters."[16]

It is a sign that our age is characterized by the struggle among principles born in the distant past that a latter-day Gassendi has arisen to recommend Peiresc as a model of "learned sociability" and as a pattern for the intellectual life.[17] Yet he cannot be a model for anyone who believes the mind to have an end beyond the enjoyment of its own exercise. For what Gassendi's *Life* and Naudé's library both represented was a rejection of the hierarchy of knowledge. In other tracts of the Renaissance, such as Léon Battista Alberti's *On Painting*, Machiavelli's *Prince*, and Galileo's *Two New Sciences*, individual pursuits had been declared to be autonomous, that is, neither ordered to nor directed by the truths contemplated by metaphysics and theology. In the works of Naudé and Gassendi, the practices and goals of the humanistic scholarly life as a whole were similarly set free. To their conception of the new learning, the virtue of studiousness was entirely irrelevant, because there was no hierarchy of studies and, consequently, there could be no harm in choosing the lower over the higher. At best, the new learning occasionally acknowledged the need for a kind of moderation in the pursuit of knowledge akin to the Epicurean's care not to gorge himself. For the desire to know had become merely another passion of the soul, to be enjoyed in its operation like any other. Curiosity was no longer a vice, it had become the name of the passion. On this point, as on many others, it was Montaigne who summed up his age: "When the mind is satisfied, that is a sign of diminished faculties or weariness."[18]

---

16. Pierre Bayle edited the *Nouvelles de la République des Lettres* from 1684–87. On these developments, see Jonathan I. Israel, *Radical Enlightenment: Philosophy and the Making of Modernity, 1650-1750* (New York: Oxford University Press, 2001), 119–55.

17. See Peter N. Miller, *Peiresc's Europe: Learning and Virtue in the Seventeenth Century* (New Haven: Yale University Press, 2000).

18 Montaigne, "On Experience," in *The Essays: A Selection*, trans. M. A. Screech (London: Penguin, 1993), 368.

Bossuet's Witness to the Virtue of Studiousness

The Christian mind thirsts not for the endless quest, but for the peace of resting in God. "For now we see in a mirror dimly, but then face to face. Now I know in part; then I shall understand fully." (1 Cor. 13:12) There was a promise of limitless knowledge in that first temptation, and similar chimeras have led countless souls astray through the ages. The most clear-sighted of Christian teachers, therefore, have always followed St. Paul in seeing the mind as a glorious but unruly gift. Our "every thought" is to be taken "captive to obey Christ" (2 Cor. 2:5); we are to be "renewed in the spirit of our minds" (Eph. 4:23). In his convictions about knowledge and learning, Bossuet was a student of St. Paul. In chronicling his witness to the virtue of studiousness, it is necessary first to sketch the outlines of his life of study, then to consider his assessment of the threats posed by the new learning, before at last turning to his prescriptions for the right ordering of the desire to know.

Like his contemporary Molière, whose nemesis he was, Bossuet was formed by the *Ratio Studiorum*, at a Jesuit school in his hometown of Dijon.[19] His youth there was a serious one, as tended to be the case with the sons of the French judicial nobility. When he was eleven, his father was appointed a judge in Metz, and Bossuet was left in Dijon in the home of his uncle, also a judge, and a formidable figure who made his nephew memorize verses of Virgil beyond those he was required to learn at school. It was in his uncle's library that Bossuet happened upon the Latin text of the Bible and thus, at fourteen, began a lifelong devotion to the Word of God. He left Dijon for Paris when he was fifteen, and passed from success to success, ending with his recognition as Doctor of the Sorbonne and his ordination to the priesthood, both in the spring of 1652. Already by his early twenties he had been introduced to the Republic of Letters in Paris at its twin poles, the fashionable Hôtel Rambouillet and the learned cabinet or study of the brothers Dupuy—frequented by Gabriel Naudé, among others—to which

---

19. On Bossuet's education, see Thérèse Goyet, *L'Humanisme de Bossuet*, 2 vols. (Paris: Klinckseick, 1965), I: 3–44.

he had been recommended for his "taste for belles-lettres," "grace," and "ability to speak in public."[20] A recent biographer has tried to see Bossuet as a "worldly young cleric" who knew firsthand the attractions of Parisian society.[21] The documentary evidence that remains from this period of his life offers scant support for such a view. The "Meditation on the Brevity of Life" that he wrote on the eve of his ordination to the diaconate in 1648 bespoke an elevated piety and treated the sins of youth in conventional terms: "What then remains to me? Of lawful pleasures, a useless memory, of unlawful, a regret, a debt owed to Hell or to penance."[22] In any event, the imposing achievements of his youth suggest that dissipation was never his flaw.

Adequately to take the measure of Bossuet's mind would be a lengthy task. As an indication of its qualities, however, it may be helpful to note the parallels between him and John Henry Newman. For all of the inevitable differences between one man rooted in the soil of Catholic France and another who spent half of his life discovering the Catholic Church, the similarities of their minds are striking. Each man was educated in the Classics, read and wrote Latin as if it were his mother tongue, and had a mind shaped by Virgil and Cicero. Each also mastered Greek. They were immersed in the writings of the Fathers of the Church; Bossuet was more indebted to St. Augustine, Newman to the Cappadocians, but both were Patristic in their sensibilities. Both were incomparable prose stylists, who composed effortlessly and powerfully in their native languages, whose respective geniuses each lifted to new heights. Both were men of letters who kept abreast of the learned world, wrote works of controversy to stem the tide of what they perceived to be dangerous innovation, and were often consulted by their peers and regarded as trustworthy judges in

---

20. Letter of Nicolas Rigault to the Brothers Dupuy, April 3, 1650, in *Correspondance de Bossuet*, nouvelle édition, eds. Ch. Urbain and E. Levesque (Paris: Hachette, 1909), I: 417.

21. Georges Minois, *Bossuet: Entre Dieu et le Soleil* (Paris: Perrin, 2003), 39.

22. Bossuet, *Méditation sur la Brièveté de la Vie*, in *Oeuvres Oratoires*, édition critique de J. Lebarq, revue et augmentée par Ch. Urbain et E. Levesque, 7 volumes (Paris: Desclée, 1926), I:11.

matters aesthetic, moral, and theological. Both were lifelong church-men who understood that their significant talents had been entrusted to them that they might make a serious use of them in service to the people of God. Both were critics of the new learning and educators charged with transmitting the old. Both, finally, had minds trained always to look to the end by the careful study of the works of Aristotle.

Just as some of the most piercing phrases in Newman's work are to be found in the *Parochial and Plain Sermons* of his Anglican years, so also is Bossuet's genius visible in the sermons he delivered from his late twenties to his early forties, when he was a Canon of Metz and occasional preacher before the Royal Court. From his panegyric of St. Joseph (1656), his charge "On the Eminent Dignity of the Poor in the Church," (1659) and his "Sermon on Death" preached at Court during his Lenten series in 1662, to what is often said to be his masterpiece, his funeral oration for the Duchess of Orléans (1670), he composed a series of great works that secured his reputation as one of the most eloquent preachers in an age that cultivated refined taste in oratory. Few were published during his life, but since his death they have been endlessly reprinted and anthologized and are still studied in French schools today. Themes such as the hatred of the truth by free-think-ers and the necessity of preaching the Word of God are widespread among them. In one sermon in particular, however, the vice of curios-ity forms the entire subject, a panegyric of St. Catherine of Alexandria first preached by him in 1660.

Bossuet's exposition began with a commonplace. "Knowledge" is one of "heaven's gifts," but it is often "spoiled in our hands by the use that we make of it." The body of the sermon consisted in three points, divided according to a passage from one of St. Bernard's ser-mons on the Song of Songs. St. Bernard had identified three vices stemming from the improper pursuit of knowledge: curiosity, in those who seek to know "only that they might know;" vanity, in those who would know that they might be admired; and greed, in those who would know that they might become rich. Bossuet set the example of St. Catherine against these vices—all forms of curiosity on Aquinas's accounting—showing in each case that right intention was the crucial cause of the proper regulation of the desire to know. Thus to "the curious," who "fatten themselves with fruitless and idle speculation," he explained that the "light" of knowledge was not given "only that you might enjoy seeing it" but to "conduct your steps and rule your will." Christ is to be the ultimate object of our knowledge, and not merely as the truth, but also as "the way." The vain he reminded that truth does not "belong to us," for it is a gift from on high and it is destined for the service of others. Like St. Paul, we are not to "show forth our knowledge" for any other purpose than "to make known Jesus Christ." And he placed before the avaricious, who study theology merely to gain a benefice, the example of St. Catherine, who "consecrated" her knowledge "uniquely to the salvation of souls." The sermon concluded on a note of evangelical zeal: "And so, my brothers, may everyone preach the Gospel, in his family, among his friends, in his conversation . . . and may each of us make use of all his lights to win souls entangled by the world and to make the holy truth of God reign upon the earth."[23]

Bossuet's sermons often convey a similar sense of urgency, and especially on the subject of knowledge. The age of St. Vincent de Paul, the Jesuit martyrs of North America, and the Trappist reform was also the age of Montaigne and Peiresc, Molière and Naudé. There was a war being waged for the soul of France, with the "science of the saints" set against a "false wisdom, which, shutting itself within the walls of mortal things, entombs itself with them in nothingness."[24] Bossuet was not alone in seeing the danger. Pascal, whom he admired, inveighed against the tendency of the age to pursue "the bustle which distracts and amuses us" and saw in an "uneasy curiosity" the "chief malady" of mankind.[25] And the poet Racine came to see more harm than good in the world of letters, urging his son to form his mind by "rereading his Cicero" and warning him not to let his love for French books "inspire

23. Bossuet, "Panegyrique de Sainte Catherine," *Oeuvres Oratoires*, ed. Urbain et Levesque, III: 548–74.

24. Bossuet, "Sainte Catherine," III: 552, and "Oraison funèbre de la Duchesse d'Orléans," (1670) *Oeuvres Oratoires*, V: 661.

25. Pascal, *Pensées*, #s 168, 618, trans. Honor Levi (New York: Oxford University Press, 1995), 45, 136.

in him a distaste for more useful reading, especially that of works of piety and morals."[26] To Bossuet, the snares for the Christian mind were many. In an age of great preachers, there was the possibility of letting the ears be "flattered by the cadence and arrangement of the words" and failing to let "wisdom walk in front as mistress, eloquence behind as servant."[27] In an age of antiquarians and philologists, an "insatiable desire to know history" was emerging; some were even daring to treat "Jesus Christ as a subject for the inquiry of the curious."[28] In circles in which piety had become fashionable, some read the Port-Royal Bible "more on account of the translators than of the God who is speaking."[29] In an age when theological controversies were the common coin of the chattering classes, there was the danger of allowing oneself to be "carried off by the desire to know" in the premature reading of theological works.[30] In each of these errors or excesses there was a common denominator of rebellion, sometimes subtle, sometimes open, against the order of Divine wisdom. For "our reason," Bossuet once explained in a letter to a close friend, "is reason only to the extent to which it is submitted to God."[31]

The vision that recognizes the characteristic faults of the age is valuable, but still more so is the one that perceives the true excellence of virtue. Bossuet was not merely a critic of curiosity, nor even a theorist of studiousness, he was a defender and exemplar of the virtue. In his expression of the ideal, his elaboration of its practices, and his own pursuit of wisdom there are what may be called three notes or

---

26. Racine's letters to his son of October 14, 1693, and October 3, 1694, in *Oeuvres Complètes*, II: *Prose*, ed. Raymond Picard (Paris: Gallimard, 1966), 540 and 552.

27. Bossuet, "Sermon sur la Parole de Dieu," (1661) in *Oeuvres Oratoires*, III: 626–27 (echoing Augustine's *On Christian Doctrine*).

28. *Traité de la Concupiscence* (first published posthumously in 1731), in *Oeuvres Complètes de Bossuet*, ed. Abbé Guillaume, ten volumes (Lyon: Briday, 1879), IX: 554; "Panégyrique du Bienheureux François de Sales," (1660) in *Oeuvres Oratoires*, III: 578.

29. Bossuet to the Maréchal de Bellefonds, Letter of December 1, 1674, in *Correspondance*, I: 334.

30. Bossuet to Bellefonds, Letter of July 7, 1673, in *Correspondance*, I:293.

31. Bossuet to Bellefonds, Letter of February 8, 1674, in *Correspondance*, I: 307.

properties of Christian studiousness: the necessity of moral virtue for the search for truth, fidelity to the tradition of the Church, and the ordination of knowledge to the common good.

Bossuet set forth studiousness as an ideal in his funeral oration for his mentor, Nicolas Cornet, Doctor of the Sorbonne. As Grand-Maître of the theology faculty, Cornet was responsible for having drawn the famous "Five Propositions" from Cornelius Jansen's *Augustinus* that formed the basis of the ecclesiastical and royal censures of Jansenism and were a source of controversy for decades. The oration paints a portrait of a Christian scholar almost the precise opposite of Gassendi's *Life of Peiresc*. Cornet was just as selflessly devoted to his studies as the Provençal antiquary had been, but added ascetic practices to single-mindedness. Bossuet lauded his innocence and modesty, his rejection of luxury and his generosity to the poor, and—unheard of excellence—his steadfast refusal of preferment. "Imitate his virtues, practice humility as he did, love obscurity as he loved it." Unlike Peiresc, Cornet checked his desire for knowledge and made it serve the Church. "The first duty of a man who studies sacred truths," Bossuet explained, "is to know how to distinguish the places where it is permissible to enter from those where we must stop short, and to remember the narrow limits by which our intellect is bounded." The wise man knows how to "moderate the fire of that restless mobility that causes in us that intemperance and sickness of knowing, and to be wise soberly and according to measure." Cornet, accordingly, shunned "refined chicanery and the subtlety of vain distinctions" and instead devoted himself to St. Augustine, whom he held to be the "most enlightened and profound of all the doctors," and also to "the school of St. Thomas." His fidelity to the tradition of the Church was matched by his spirit of service. He "consecrated his understanding to the Faith and his memory to the eternal memory of God," and spoke as an oracle and with gravity amidst the tumult of the dispute over grace, when he was "consulted by all of France." In sum, this "hidden treasure" was also a "public treasure."[32]

---

32. "Orasion funèbre de Nicolas Cornet," (1663) *Oeuvres Oratoires*, IV: 470–93. On Cornet's influence upon Bossuet, see LeBrun, *Spiritualité de Bossuet*, 42-46. Bossu-

With less eloquence and insistence upon the moral virtues, but with greater precision about the intellectual life, Bossuet composed two brief treatises for clerical protégés, which, taken together, provide a summary of his views on theological education. The first was a treatise written in 1670 for the young Cardinal de Bouillon, "On Style and the Reading of the Fathers of the Church for the formation of an Orator." Here Bossuet wrote with sovereign confidence about the means by which to attain a "figurative" and "ornate" style. Demosthenes in the Greek and Cicero in the Latin were his models. From the "few books" he had read in French, he recommended those by Pascal and Racine, but like Racine, counseled that reading in the vernacular was to be done "without abandoning other, serious reading; one or two pieces suffice to give an idea" of the style. Far more important, even for "forming style" was to "understand the thing, to penetrate the basis and the end of it all," which was to be done by "knowing very well" the Old and New Testaments. Here, too, he warned against a certain excessive curiosity: "I have learned by experience that when one attaches oneself stubbornly to penetrating the obscure passages instead of passing them by, one wastes on difficult questions time that should have been spent reflecting upon what is clear, which is what forms the mind and nourishes piety." The Fathers, finally, were the essential guides, and among them, St. Augustine and St. John Chrysostom: "The former raises the mind to great and subtle considerations, and the latter draws it back and fits it to the capacity of the people." To the theological treatises of Augustine and the sermons of Chrysostom, he added St. Gregory the Great's *Pastoral Rule*, explaining that "these works" were to be read "for the sake of forming a body of doctrine."[33]

---

et's oration was not published in his lifetime, and its textual integrity has been questioned. Jean Calvet, for instance, declined to place it in the same company as the later and more famous funeral orations, reckoning Bossuet's praise for Cornet as cast in "conventional terms." Calvet, *Bossuet: l'homme et l'oeuvre* (Paris: Hatier-Boivin, 1941), 10. It is to be noted that Urbain and Levesque concluded with "certitude" that the "discourse as a whole belonged to Bossuet, though there were reserves to be made about the details." *Oeuvres Oratoires*, IV: 471.

33. "Sur le Style, et la lecture des Pères de l'Eglise pour former un orateur," *Oeuvres Oratoires*, VII: 13-20.

Five years later, Bossuet's counsel took the form of a letter "On the Studies that ought to follow the Licentiate." Here again, for a different clerical student and at greater length, he sketched a program of reading Holy Scripture and the Fathers of the Church. The treatise is significant for containing a statement of Bossuet's understanding of the academic forms of his day. The studies for the licentiate he held to be strictly preliminary; they were "exercises for disputation" that instructed in a "few questions" but did not "compose a body of doctrine." At that level, the ancient texts of the Fathers were read only in extracts, and therefore gave only "slim and confused knowledge." With one's licentiate behind him, the student could devote more time to the "reading of the ancients," that he might "penetrate their sentiments and attempt to conciliate them, and, finally, to search for the tradition of the Church." This experience of apprenticeship to the Fathers is what "properly makes a body of doctrine and merits the quality of doctor." It is what allows the student to "give an account, on each dogma and question, of what was the sentiment of the Fathers of the Church."[34] What is crucial to note here is that Bossuet understood theological studies to have a determinate end. To attain that end was a duty for a preacher, whose office was to fulfill the divine command to teach the faith: "it is the fear of judgment that makes preachers ascend into the pulpit."[35]

It was the same clarity about the end of studies that shaped Bossuet's years as tutor of Louis XIV's son, the Grand Dauphin. Bossuet described his aims and practices in a letter to Pope Innocent XI, which he composed towards the end of his tenure. *De Institutione Ludovici Delphini* deserves to be placed in a select company of Christian pedagogical works, and might fruitfully be compared to St. Basil's *Address to Young Men on Reading Greek Literature.* Just as St. Basil exhorted his hearers to attend first to the "care of the soul," so also Bossuet made

---

34. "Ecrit de Bossuet sur les études qui doivent suivre la licence," ed. E. Levesque, *Revue Bossuet* 1 (1900): 14.

35. "Sur la Prédication Evangélique," (1662) *Oeuvres Oratoires*, IV: 177. The comment was based upon II Corinthians 5:10–11.

the three words piety, goodness, and justice the "principles" to which he referred "everything that we have given [the Dauphin]. He saw that everything came from this source, that everything tended to that point, and that his studies had no other object than to make him able to acquit himself of all of his duties with ease."[36] In his catechism and elementary religious instruction, the Dauphin learned "to love Jesus Christ; to embrace him in his infancy, to grow with him, obeying his parents and making himself agreeable to God and to man." After having "read and reread the Gospels," he passed to the Old Testament, and, for "diversion," to the lives of the Fathers and Martyrs. In his study of grammar, he was made to read pagan authors, but "without ever straying from our design, which was to hand on piety and good morals at the same time as civil prudence." To this end the Dauphin read many historical works, but he was not allowed to "descend into minutiae or follow curiosities," rather he concentrated on the study of customs and laws and exemplars of the craft of kingship, especially St. Louis, "the greatest exemplar of kings."[37] In sum, in the words of Thérèse Goyet, "never was a single subject, at any moment, studied without a view of its ends."[38]

In his own life as a scholar Bossuet conformed to the practices he recommended and imposed upon his royal charge. Like many great preachers and scholars and countless contemplatives through the ages, his mind was formed by Sacred Scripture, which he knew from memory. He took with the utmost seriousness the call to submit his own mind to that of the Fathers, whom he read systematically in the 1650s as a canon of Metz, again in the 1670s, and for a third time later in life in response to the challenge of Biblical criticism.[39] Perhaps only a celibate could really hope to imitate his single-mindedness and indus-

---

36. St. Basil, *Address to Young Men on the Reading of Greek Literature*, in Anton Pegis, ed., *The Wisdom of Catholicism* (New York: Random House, 1949), 20. Bossuet, *De Institutione Ludovici Delphini, Oeuvres Complètes*, VII: 348.

37. *De Institutione Ludovici Delphini, Oeuvres Complètes*, VII: 347–54.

38. Goyet, *L'Humanisme de Bossuet*, II: 103.

39. See the comments of Jean Calvet, *La littérature religieuse de François de Sales à Fénelon* (Paris: Editions Mondiales, 1956), 265–66, 278–79.

try; it seems probable that, like Newman, he was capable of reading with attention for upwards of eight hours a day.[40] What makes Bossuet more approachable and even a relevant model is the decade he spent as the Dauphin's primary instructor. All through his forties, this orator of consummate mastery revisited the texts that had formed him in his youth, taking an indifferent student line-by-line through Caesar and Virgil. The *Discourse on Universal History* remains as a testament to the benefits that accrued to Bossuet from his rereading and teaching, and his funeral oration for the Prince de Condé amply proves that his eloquence did not suffer from the trial.

In an age when partisans of the new learning such as Gabriel Naudé and Pierre Gassendi were advancing the ideal of a life spent in the limitless pursuit of any sort of knowledge whatever and assisting in the creation of institutions dedicated to that project, Jacques-Bénigne Bossuet defended the necessity of restraint in the pursuit of truth and dedicated himself to the perpetuation of the traditional practices of Christian studiousness. Today, heirs to Naudé, Gassendi, and Peiresc speak freely of their role in what is called knowledge-making. Those who believe that the mind is a gift given to us that we might come to know God may well suspect, as Paul Griffiths has argued, that the "intellectual appetites" demanded by "the contemporary academy" are "corrupt," and that fidelity to the Catholic intellectual tradition demands the recovery of practices of "religious reading."[41] The example of Bossuet can provide some markers for the path to that recovery. First, his awareness that curiosity was an imminent and serious danger is itself instructive. Without our critical reflection, the structures of contemporary academic culture will continue to encourage individual scholars to pursue their private career goals in such a way as to make curiosity and narrow specialization a more likely result of their endeavors than studiousness and wisdom. Second, Bossuet's counsel

---

40. Newman's diaries recording the details of his studies are reproduced in Volume I of *The Letters and Diaries of John Henry Newman*, eds. Ian Ker and Thomas Gornall, S.J. (Oxford: Clarendon Press, 1978).

41. Paul J. Griffiths, "The Vice of Curiosity," *Pro Ecclesia* 15 (2006): 48.

and practice of the reverent rereading of Sacred Scripture and apprenticeship to the Fathers of the Church provides a vivid model of the restraint that is studiousness. The desire to know can be properly restrained only when it is properly directed, when we most keenly seek the best and highest kind of knowledge, putting in the second place or even setting aside knowledge of lower things. For Bossuet, the duty to preach and to teach the Faith kept his life of studies rightly ordered. Yet as the Dauphin's tutor, he was forced to return to those elementary subjects and subordinate sciences that occupy much of our attention and which indeed need to be mastered before one is ready to ascend to higher subjects. Bossuet's pedagogical principles and practices show that even in the lower subjects, he kept his sight trained on those which are above, and thus was true to Hugh of St. Victor's saying that "our objective" in our learning "ought to be always to keep ascending."[42]

---

42. *The Didascalicon of Hugh of St. Victor: A Medieval Guide to the Arts*, trans. Jerome Taylor (New York: Columbia University Press, 1961), 133.

3

A Fruitful Restraint

IN THE HALF-CENTURY SINCE the opening of the Second Vatican Council, Catholic colleges and universities in America have been the setting of one long argument about the nature and purpose of education. The discussion has been increasingly poignant in recent years, as it has become difficult to ignore not only the secularization of Catholic higher education, but its intellectual and pedagogical poverty as well.[1] The latest contribution to this conversation comes from an historian, Brad S. Gregory, who has portrayed the secularization of the Catholic university as the ironic and unintentional result of the papal promotion of Thomism. Gregory does not blame any defect in the thought of Aquinas, but instead points to a concomitant attribute as Thomism's tragic flaw, the "papal suspicion of scientific and historical knowledge-making." The cultural revolution that swept through Catholic faculties in the 1960s, on his account, involved the rejection of Thomism as a by-product of the "intellectual catching-up" that Catholic universities had to do. During this transformation, the "neo-Thomist subcul-

---

1. Notably elegiac on both counts is Alasdair MacIntyre's "The End of Education: The Fragmentation of the American University," *Commonweal* (October 20, 2006): 10–14. See also the symposium on MacIntyre's *God, Philosophy, Universities* in the Fall 2011 number of the English edition of *Nova et Vetera* (volume 9), especially Thomas Hibbs, "The Research University in Crisis (Again): MacIntyre's *God, Philosophy, Universities*," pp. 947–66, which includes a helpful retrospective back to John Tracy Ellis and the debates of the 1950s.

ture" was swept away at least in part because of its "timidity in the face of knowledge-making by secularizing research universities."[2] As an explanation of the wholesale jettisoning of Thomistic philosophy and theology at Catholic colleges and universities, the account is a familiar one and not implausible.[3] It is possible to point to bold attempts on the part of leading Thomists to breathe new life into the tradition, such as Charles de Koninck's 1964 Medalist Address at the annual meeting of the American Catholic Philosophical Association and Ralph McInerny's 1966 spirited tract *Thomism in an Age of Renewal*.[4] Yet these do seem to stand as exceptions to a general trend of retreat in the face of a confident and aggressive rival ideal: the Berlin-style research university.[5]

Gregory's judgment seems to repose upon two principles: that all knowledge of the truth is good, and that to attain it requires fortitude because its pursuit involves arduous work of reflection, investigation, argumentation, and even public debate. Both principles are unquestionably true, and their relevance to Catholic intellectual life has been continually reaffirmed in recent years in such authoritative statements as St. John Paul II's *Fides et Ratio* and Benedict XVI's celebrated Regensburg Address. The characterization of the development of educational institutions and practices over time, however, seems likely to benefit from an additional weighing of the principles of judgment. In particular, the prominence of the word "timidity" in Gregory's ac-

---

2. Brad S. Gregory, *The Unintended Reformation: How a Religious Revolution Secularized Society* (Cambridge, Massachusetts: Harvard University Press, 2012), 360–64.

3. Gregory notes his debt to the standard narrative: Philip Gleason, *Contending with Modernity: Catholic Higher Education in the Twentieth Century* (New York: Oxford University Press, 1995). Like Gregory, Gleason located the problem in the neighborhood of a defect in fortitude, using the word "malaise" to describe the loss of confidence in Thomism that developed through the 1960s.

4. Charles de Koninck, "Three Sources of Philosophy," Proceedings of the ACPA 38 (1964):13–22; Ralph M. McInerny, *Thomism in an Age of Renewal* (1966; reprinted Notre Dame: University of Notre Dame Press, 1968).

5. See George M. Marsden, *The Soul of the American University: From Protestant Establishment to Established Nonbelief* (New York: Oxford University Press, 1994), especially chapter 5: "American Practicality and Germanic Ideals: Two Visions for Reform."

count invites several questions in reply. May not a charge of timidity at times stem from the prosecutor's failure to recognize prudent restraint? Is courage the only or even the chief virtue governing the search for truth? Is there a role for temperance in the intellectual life, that is, for the wise moderation of the desire to know? Questions such as these are not only relevant to the task of constructing a convincing historical narrative, they also point to matters of enduring relevance to the pursuit of truth.

Among the many effects of the secularization of the modern university, one has been a growing awareness that its institutional forms and practices and the habits that they inculcate ought not simply be taken at face value by Catholics, but should be evaluated in light of an understanding of a healthy "intellectual custom."[6] Jan Aertsen, for instance, has affirmed that there is a Thomistic "ethic of knowing," while Thomas Hibbs has suggested that we ought to "conceive of the full range of our activities, including intellectual activities, as practices, involving a host of relevant virtues."[7] It is within just such a general understanding of the virtues of the intellectual life that claims about "timidity" or proper restraint in the face of "knowledge-making" can be usefully considered. Our present purpose is to explore a line of investigation into the topic, by taking note of two contemporary accounts of right intellectual appetite and then reflecting upon Aquinas's conception of the virtue of studiousness.

In the context of an ambitious attempt to understand the virtues of the intellectual life, philosophers R. C. Roberts and W. J. Wood have identified a virtue they call the "love of knowledge," defining it as a habit of inquiry in which knowledge is desired for its "significance, relevance, and worthiness."[8] With more focused attention, Paul

---

6. The phrase is Ronald McArthur's; see his "Saint Thomas and the Formation of the Catholic Mind," in *The Ever-Illuminating Wisdom of St. Thomas Aquinas* (San Francisco: Ignatius Press, 1999), 123–43.

7. Jan Aertsen, "Aquinas and the Human Desire for Knowledge," ACPQ 79 (2005): 415; Thomas Hibbs, *Aquinas, Ethics, and Philosophy of Religion: Metaphysics and Practice* (Bloomington, IN: Indiana University Press, 2007), 36.

8. Robert C. Roberts and W. Jay Wood, *Intellectual Virtues: An Essay in Regulative Epistemology* (New York: Oxford University Press, 2007), 155.

Griffiths has explored the subject in his study *Intellectual Appetite: A Theological Grammar*, where he notes that while for many today the "appetite for knowledge is an undifferentiated good," to the "long Christian tradition" it has been regarded as an appetite that needed to be "catechized and disciplined" like any other. Griffiths' proposal for how it should be disciplined centers on a distinction between the seeking of knowledge for ownership as a private possession and the seeking of knowledge for the sake of what he calls "reflexive intimacy with the gift."[9] What is initially noteworthy about these accounts is that they agree on two essential starting points: that knowledge, as such, is a good, but that the seeking of it can be either well or poorly integrated into human life as a whole. Like any other appetite, the desire to know needs to be brought under the measure of some rule.

Might the desire for knowledge, however, be capable of providing that measure for itself, that is, of autonomy? Consider St. Jerome's counsel: "Love the knowledge of the Scriptures, and you will not love the vices of the flesh."[10] Although St. Jerome's reference to the particular reading material—Sacred Scripture—was surely not accidental, many others have seen in liberal studies themselves a kind of pleasure that is wholly honorable and even morally beneficial in itself, whatever the object of study. The premise lies just beneath the surface in a recent volume by Stanley Fish, who affirms that "sustained inquiry into the truth of a matter . . . improves you" and, without irony, characterizes the task of undergraduate instruction as "to initiate students into the pleasures of an academic life," as though this phrase named an unequivocal good.[11] Another recent investigation of the intellectual virtues values "inquisitiveness" and a "deep and abiding desire for knowledge" as long as the knowledge is being sought for its own sake rather than for worldly gain; on this view, an appetite for knowledge is virtuous if it is "a posi-

---

9. Paul J. Griffiths, *Intellectual Appetite: A Theological Grammar* (Washington, DC: The Catholic University of America Press, 2009), see esp. 1–18.

10. St. Jerome as quoted in St. Thomas Aquinas, *Contra Impugnantes Dei Cultum et Religionem*, III.4.ad 4.

11. Stanley Fish, *Save the World on Your Own Time* (New York: Oxford University Press, 2008), 40, 164.

tive psychological orientation toward epistemic goods."[12] That such a conception would be prevalent is not surprising; Aquinas, after all, affirmed that "spiritual pleasures, strictly speaking, are in accordance with reason, wherefore they need no control." Yet his analysis did not stop there; he added this crucial qualification: "save accidentally, in so far as one spiritual pleasure is a hindrance to another."[13] Certainly it is well to recall in this context Newman's celebrated affirmation that knowledge by itself does not supply virtue: "Quarry the granite rock with razors, or moor the vessel with a thread of silk; then you may hope with such keen and delicate instruments as human knowledge and human reason to contend against those giants, the passion and the pride of man."[14] The real difficulty here lies in establishing that some forms of intellectual satisfaction are more fitting than others and hence more worthy of pursuit. Roberts and Wood admit that "different moral and metaphysical communities will promote different versions" of the virtue they call "the love of knowledge," and seemingly regret to think that rival claims can be assessed "only by a sort of metaphysical adjudication which is in all probability unavailable to human beings."[15] Griffiths, for his part, enunciates the principle on the basis of which the value of different kinds of knowledge can be weighed, affirming that "a hierarchy in the order of being has an accompanying difference in the order of knowing," but does not employ the principle as the basis for his own theory of the virtue of studiousness.[16]

---

12. Jason Baehr, *The Inquiring Mind* (New York: Oxford University Press, 2011), 91, 93, 102. Baehr's earlier formulation should also be noted (p. 19): "A person with the virtue of curiosity, or whose mental life is characterized by wonder, is quick to notice and be inclined to investigate issues or subject matters of significance."

13. *Summa Theologiae* II-II, 141.4.ad 4. Dominican Fathers translation.

14. John Henry Newman, *The Idea of a University*, ed. Martin J. Svaglic (Notre Dame: University of Notre Dame Press, 1982), 91. For a further development of the point, see his "Tamworth Reading Room."

15. Roberts and Wood, *Intellectual Virtues*, 180.

16. Griffiths, *Intellectual Appetite*, 39. As an example of his subsequent analysis, this passage is characteristic (p. 138): "The *cotoneaster adpressus* [a shrub], the Messiaen prelude, the face of the human other, the ensemble of desire and institutional form that constitutes the economic order—all these, if approached as the studious do, yield themselves in part to the intimacy-seeking knower's gaze."

Even according to natural reason, an account of the measure of intellectual appetite that does not take our knowledge of God as its ultimate standard cannot be found satisfactory by those who earnestly seek knowledge of the causes of things. For, as Catholic philosophers have recently been reminded by Alasdair MacIntyre, "to be a theist is to understand every particular as . . . pointing towards God" and "to hold that all explanation and understanding that does not refer to God both as first cause and as final end is incomplete."[17] What is needed is an account of the virtue of studiousness that asks the radical question: with respect to what ultimate measure can the different kinds of knowledge be judged?[18] We need, therefore, nothing less than Aquinas's own account.

Studiousness, according to Saint Thomas, is a potential part of the virtue of temperance, a secondary virtue, as it were, that enables one to have "a right desire to apply the power of knowing, in this way rather than in another, and to this rather than to that."[19] Although the virtue gains its name, studiousness, from the student's application to his subject, its nature is clearly on the side of moderation rather than intensification: "studiousness," Aquinas explains, "consists in restraint, and that is why it is located as a part of temperance." Now, it is helpful to be told that, like temperance itself, studiousness is a kind of restraint, a bridling of appetite by reason's rule, but the *content* of that rule is what we are seeking. Augustine's teaching that "to be curious is prohibited," provided in the *sed contra* of the same article, suggests

17. Alasdair MacIntyre, "On Being a Theistic Philosopher in a Secularized Culture," *Proceedings of the ACPA* 84 (2011): 23.

18. For an analysis of studiousness proceeding from the same question, see McInerny, *Thomism in an Age of Renewal*, 124–29; and for an admonition about the importance of asking radical questions about rival conceptions of the virtues, see David Solomon, "Virtue Ethics: Radical or Routine?," in Michael DePaul and Linda Zagzebski, eds., *Intellectual Virtue: Perspectives from Ethics and Epistemology* (Oxford: Clarendon Press, 2003), 57–80.

19. *Summa Theologiae* II-II, 166.2.ad 2. For another discussion of the virtue, see Gregory Reichberg, "Studiositas, the Virtue of Attention," in Daniel McInerny, ed., *The Common Things: Essays on Thomism and Education* (Washington, DC: Maritain Association, 1999), 143–52.

that the kinds of moderation effected by studiousness will be revealed through its opposition to the vice of curiosity.

In his discussion of curiosity, Aquinas identifies four ways in which the knowledge of the truth can be immoderately desired.[20] First, when the study of something "less useful" draws one away from "what one is obliged" to study, as, for instance, in the case of a preacher who prefers the poets to the prophets. Second, when one wishes to learn from an illicit teacher, as by divination. Third, when someone "desires to know the truth about creatures without referring it to its due end, that is, to the knowledge of God." And fourth, when "someone seeks knowledge of the truth beyond the capacity of his own mind," which, Aquinas points out, is problematic because to do so is to court error. His teaching may be summarized in a series of positive injunctions: the studious man desires to learn about those things his state in life obliges him to know, from the right teachers, referring his knowledge of created things to God as their principle and end, and, finally, desires to study subjects he is actually able to understand.

Let us now make a fresh start by considering how Aquinas's prescription speaks to our contemporary needs, indeed to the perennial needs of the search for truth. As studiousness is a part of the virtue of temperance, it will be well to begin by considering the ordination of temperance to other goods. It is, to be sure, essentially ordered to higher spiritual goods, beginning with the virtue of fortitude, but it is also and most evidently productive of the well-being of the body, whose passions it rectifies. The bodily good that we chiefly expect from temperance is health, together with its companions, beauty and strength (making provision, of course, for the different seasons of our lives). Something analogous would seem to obtain for studiousness. The mind whose desire for knowledge is rightly ordered ought, all things being equal, to be strong, beautiful, and healthy. Is it too much to suppose, then, that we might consider the virtue of studiousness to be ordered to the flourishing of those characteristics that make the

---

20. *Summa Theologiae* II-II, 167.1

mind strong, beautiful, and healthy, that is, to the intellectual virtues? In what follows, each intellectual virtue will be considered from the perspective of its relationship to intellectual appetite, and as reposing upon a kind of restraint or disciplined practice of learning and communicating the fruits of learning.

The Path That Leads to Wisdom

The injunction that the student should most desire to study what he is capable of understanding seems unambiguously to point to Aquinas's account of the order of learning and thus to the need to acquire the liberal arts and speculative sciences as permanent habits of mind and to acquire them in the proper order.[21] The injunction, after all, cannot mean that we are meant to remain in whatever intellectual condition we find ourselves, for, as Newman once memorably said, "it is impossible to stop the growth of a mind."[22] Indeed any desire to study is a desire to improve, as even a desire to gain a better and more enduring hold upon what one already knows is itself a kind of improvement. Our appetite for knowledge, therefore, must be ruled by a standard that permits and directs its growth, which is just what is promised by the order of learning, the "path that leads to wisdom."[23] That order

---

21. The essential texts from Aquinas's commentaries on the *Book of Causes* and the *Nicomachean Ethics* are conveniently printed as an appendix to Thomas Aquinas, *The Division and Methods of the Sciences*, 4th edition, trans. Armand Maurer (Toronto: Pontifical Institute of Medieval Studies, 1986), 99–102. For a recent commentary, see Leo Elders, S.V.D., "St. Thomas Aquinas on Education and Instruction," *Nova et Vetera*, English edition 7 (2009): 115–19.

22. John Henry Newman, *Loss and Gain: The Story of a Convert* [1848] (Oxford: Oxford University Press, 1986), 142.

23. John Paul II, *Fides et Ratio* (1998), §6. Although John Paul II may not have been intending a reference to the order of learning with this phrase, there are echoes of the doctrine elsewhere in the encyclical. See sections 4, 56, 60, and 81–85. For a commentary that connects the encyclical to Aquinas's account of the intellectual virtues, see Alasdair MacIntyre, "Philosophy Recalled to Its Tasks: A Thomistic reading of *Fides et Ratio*," in his *The Tasks of Philosophy: Selected Essays*, Volume 1 (Cambridge: Cambridge University Press, 2006), 186–87.

takes its form from its end, an end of which Aquinas offered this plain account: "it seems obvious that the end of any intellectual substance, even the lowest, is to understand God."[24] So, it seems that the restraint we need is not one that keeps us from climbing to the heights of that consideration, but that keeps us from doing so precipitously.[25] Just as the hiker ought to prepare to climb Mount Adams—the most rugged of the White Mountains—through a course of conditioning on lower peaks, so also the student ought not attempt to ascend to the consideration of God before taking care to strengthen his mind with the appropriate preliminary work.[26] The over-zealous hiker runs the risk of bodily injury, the presumptuous student of a mental one.

The first fruit of a desire to know that has been restrained in this way is a proper docility.[27] Just as the teacher's task is to help the student to follow the natural order of learning by pointing out the right subjects of study in the right order, so the student's is to gain the ability to distinguish between—in MacIntyre's formulation—"what is good and best for me with my particular level of training and learning in my particular circumstances to do, and what is good and best unqualifiedly."[28] Another early fruit of keeping oneself to the proper order of studies is the not inconsiderable benefit that is the sort of universal ability to judge learned discourses in terms of their method that Aristotle calls *paideia* and that Newman so effectively lauds in his

---

24. SCG III.25. For commentary, see Aertsen, "Aquinas and the Human Desire for Knowledge," 416ff.

25. *Summa Theologiae* II-II, 53.3, on the vice of precipitousness, is suggestive. The essential medieval treatment of the necessity that studies be pursued in proper order is Hugh of St. Victor's *Didascalicon*, ed. Jerome Taylor (New York: Columbia University Press, 1961).

26. For a full discussion of the subject, see Michael Augros, "The Place of Metaphysics in the Order of Learning," *The Aquinas Review* 14 (2007): 23–61.

27. Cf. *Summa Theologiae* II-II, 49.3.ad 1: "docilitas utilis sit ad quamlibet virtutem intellectualem." ("To the first then it must be said that, although docility is useful for any intellectual virtue, yet especially for prudence, for the reason already stated."

28. Alasdair MacIntyre, *Three Rival Versions of Moral Enquiry* (Notre Dame: University of Notre Dame Press, 1990), 61–62.

Idea of a University.[29] But first and more essentially, the kind of moderated desire that is involved in willingly submitting to the order of learning enables one to make good one's intellectual ground before passing on to a higher one, that is, to know the difference between what one knows and what one does not know about each subject that one is studying. The alternative is not a happy one, and has been aptly captured by Monsignor Robert Sokolowski's description of the "accidental mind." "Sheer ignorance," he writes, "is not a problem; when we are just ignorant of an issue that is raised, we know that we do not know. What is dangerous and misleading is the unselfconscious confusion of accidentals and essentials. Confused persons don't know that they don't know, but they use the names and the words associated with the things they are talking about, and so they seem to know or at least think they know what the things are."[30] The way to avoid this kind of mental confusion is by the careful training of the mind for the task of knowing, a training that involves all of the liberal arts, but among them, chiefly logic.[31]

The obstacle to gaining habitual rectitude of intellectual appetite with respect to the order of learning is that to do so seems so unappetizing. What bright university student will take freshman composition and an introductory logic class when given the chance to skip them in favor of more advanced courses, with their flashy names and interesting reading lists? How many professors are eager not only to teach the liberal arts but to help students to see that they bring desirable perfections of mind? But alas, the Pythagorean Theorem, the ablative absolute, and Barbara-Celarent are what they were many centu-

---

29. On which see Marie I. George, "The Notion of *Paideia* in Aristotle's *De Partibus Animalium*," *American Catholic Philosophical Quarterly* 67 (1993): 299–319, and MacIntyre, "The Very Idea of a University: Aristotle, Newman, and Us," *British Journal of Educational Studies* 57 (2009): 347–62.

30. Robert Sokolowski, *Phenomenology of the Human Person* (Cambridge: Cambridge University Press, 2008), 104.

31. For a recent reaffirmation of this point, see Benedict M. Ashley, O.P., *The Way toward Wisdom: An Interdisciplinary and Intercultural Introduction to Metaphysics* (Notre Dame: University of Notre Dame Press, 2006), 434-39, and especially 437.

ries ago. And so it has long been known that the tasks of teaching the liberal arts, for practical purposes, stand athwart progress in "knowledge-making." When the elective system of higher education was first proposed in the 1880s by Harvard's President Charles William Eliot, he argued that the custom of giving honors and prizes for scholarship was solely for the sake of promoting "specialization of work" and "advanced instruction." "It is unnecessary to point out," he said, "how absolutely opposed to such a policy the uniform prescription of a considerable body of elementary studies must be."[32] We are reaping the fruit of the seeds sown by Eliot. It is difficult to disagree with the lament recently penned by Columbia's Mark Taylor: "too many courses represent what the professor wants to teach rather than what students need to learn."[33]

As an initial response to Brad Gregory's charges of papal suspicion and Thomistic timidity in the face of knowledge-making, we may say, with Aquinas, that it seems reasonable to hold that one manifestation of the virtue of studiousness would be a reluctance to be satisfied with the kind of inadequate preparation of students for higher studies that an emphasis on knowledge-making seems typically to bring in its train. In the face of the cultural authority of the Berlin-style research university, to argue in favor of the liberal arts and the traditional order of the speculative disciplines may seem Quixotic. No less a committed Thomist than Alasdair MacIntyre has said that Aquinas's conception of an ordered education "was and remained a Utopian proposal."[34] In the face of such a challenge, Thomists can take consolation in the

---

32. Charles W. Eliot, "Liberty in Education," [1885] in *American Higher Education: A Documentary History*, eds. Richard Hofstadter and Wilson Smith, 2 volumes (Chicago: University of Chicago Press, 1961), 713.

33. Mark C. Taylor, *Crisis on Campus: A Bold Plan for Reforming Our Colleges and Universities* (New York: Knopf, 2010), 115.

34. MacIntyre, "Aquinas's Critique of Education: Against His Own Age, Against Ours," in *Philosophers on Education: Historical Perspectives*, ed. Amélie Oksenberg Rorty (London: Routledge, 1998), 103. But for an alternative perspective, see Reinhard Hütter, "God, the University, and the Missing Link—Wisdom: Reflections on Two Untimely Books," *The Thomist* 73 (2009): 276–77.

continuing influence of Blessed John Henry Newman, who was both the product and an eloquent proponent of just the sort of serious liberal education that the virtue of studiousness would seem to require. Although not a Thomist by training, Newman famously attested that he felt "no temptation at all to break in pieces the great legacy of thought" handed down in "the form of a science, with a method and a phraseology of its own," explicitly mentioning Aquinas as one who had given the tradition its shape.[35] Newman's own allegiance to Aristotle and his prescriptions of "elementary studies" and "discipline of mind" are well-known, and even if they are more often honored in the breach than in the observance, his status as unofficial patron of higher learning has been affirmed by Benedict XVI, and so one may perhaps be pardoned for hoping that his years of greatest influence may lie in the future.[36]

Attentiveness

It is admittedly something of an intuitive leap to see the virtue of understanding as the fruit of a suitably restrained desire to learn from the right sources and in such a way that one's learning readily refers to God as first principle and final end. It may, however, help to consider how a certain Promethean attitude coexisted with the denial of finality in the canonical founding texts of the modern mind. This is infamously the case in the works of Descartes, where we find the hope for freedom from "the infirmity of old age"—a Faustian bargain in the making if ever there were one—closely yoked to a round condemnation of the search for final causes.[37] Machiavelli was no less explicit:

---

35. John Henry Newman, *Apologia Pro Vita Sua*, ed. Ian Ker (London: Penguin, 1994), 224-25. And for commentary, see Reinhard Hütter, "Catholic Theology in America: Quo Vadis?," *Nova et Vetera*, English edition 9 (2011): 539–47.

36. See Joshua P. Hochschild, "The Re-Imagined Aristotelianism of John Henry Newman," *Modern Age* 45, (2003): 333–42 and Benedict XVI's Homily at the Mass with the Beatification of Venerable Cardinal John Henry Newman, 19 September 2010.

37. Descartes, *Discourse on Method*, VI (AT 62), and *Principles of Philosophy*, I.28 (AT

we are to dismiss inquiry into "what should be done" and turn away from "imagined republics" in order that we might instead learn from the Centaur how to "use the beast and the man."[38] But it was indeed a general trend, as technical advances were eagerly sought from such then-dubious sources as alchemical experimentation, the sketching of live nude models, and the dissection of corpses, while zeal for philosophical contemplation waned. Since it is not in artifacts, but in the works of the divine art that we chiefly encounter a goodness and intelligibility that leads us to seek their source in God, it seems unsurprising that the modern tendency to frame the intellectual life in terms of our inquiry into the various human arts would be connected to a loss of attentiveness to being and essence.

It is precisely in such an attentiveness that we can see a second element of the virtue of studiousness, which is the kind of restraint that bears fruit in the disciplining of the interior senses for the task of knowing.[39] To consider some differences between the study of nature and the study of artifacts may enable us to appreciate this restraint. In the first place, artifacts are potentially limitless and reliably novel—there is an improved Ford Mustang with every new model year—whereas the works of nature are limited and, for the most part, the same today as they were in the days of Aristotle. This potential limitlessness of artifacts seems to go together with an undirected or promiscuous fascination about them: there is always another new movie, another type of experimental painting or photography, a new direction in nouvelle cuisine. In the study of nature, by contrast, one generally encounters the order of the universe as a limit. There are, to be sure, still thousands of new beetles for us to find in the rainforest.

15–16), in *The Philosophical Writings of Descartes*, trans. John Cottingham, Robert Stoothoff, and Dugald Murdoch (Cambridge: Cambridge University Press, 1985), I:143, 202.

38. Machiavelli, *The Prince*, trans. Harvey Mansfield, 2nd edition (Chicago: University of Chicago Press, 1998), 61, 69.

39. Cf. *Summa Theologiae* I-II, 50.3.ad 3: "in interioribus viribus sensitivis apprehensivis possint poni aliqui habitus, secundum quos homo fit bene memorativus vel cogitativus vel imaginativus."

But the number of kinds of birds native to North America has long been well-known, and it is a relatively small number. Nature, moreover, loves to hide, whereas it is the characteristic of works of art to declare themselves. Even Rothko's bland canvasses make a statement. The student of nature, then, finds that his subject matter inculcates a knowledge of and respect for limits, and perhaps even a kind of natural docility and calm. It seems possible to affirm, then, that the task of knowing the being and form of natural things require a kind of looking into that makes them especially conducive to attentiveness.

The excellence that attentiveness promises is an ability to say something determinate about the natures of things. Again, Sokolowski can help us appreciate the importance of such an ability by an illustration of its opposite, a mental trait he calls "vagueness." "It is hard to imagine anyone with any intelligence," he begins, who could be "entirely devoid of insight into what trees are." But, he continues, "it is much easier to imagine that people use words like democracy, politics, freedom, and happiness, or even atom or electricity, in a vague way. The phenomenon often occurs when academics pretend to know something about quantum mechanics or Gödel's Theorem." In cases such as these, he explains, it is the "content" as well as the "form of our speech" that is "inadequate." When we are struck dumb with vagueness, he explains, it is an indication that "we do not possess the *eidos* of the thing in question."[40] But where does this vagueness come from? If the understanding of the first principles is "from nature," as Aquinas teaches, how could we come to lose or damage it except by damaging our nature?[41] There is, of course, a partial answer ready to hand in the distinction between principles known to all and those known only to the wise, a distinction that would enable us to address an example such as electricity with relative ease. But what of more universal principles, or, even the first of them all? The majesty of the fourth book of the *Metaphysics* must not be allowed to confuse us: Aristotle really did encounter sophists who not only denied the principle of contradiction

---

40. Sokolowski, *Phenomenology of the Human Person*, 149–50.

41. *Summa Theologiae* I-II, 51.1.*sed contra*.

but framed elaborate arguments in support of their denial. Theirs was a failure chiefly in the will, but there is also room for an analysis in terms of the loss or occlusion of the habit of understanding that has been provided by Aquinas: "when man ceases to make use of his intellectual habits, strange fancies, sometimes in opposition to them, arise in his imagination, so that unless those fancies be, as it were, cut off or kept back by frequent use of his intellectual habits, man becomes less fit to judge aright, and sometimes is even wholly disposed to the contrary."[42]

The obstacles that pull us away from the use of our understanding and insert "strange fancies" into our minds are legion. Consider Cardinal Ratzinger's contention that the increase in drug abuse in the West was a "warning signal" that revealed a "vacuum in our society," and an "interior longing in man which breaks out in perverted form if it does not find its true satisfaction."[43] Or again, Reinhard Hütter's observation of the connection between the consumption of pornography and the vice of acedia.[44] These examples are the most extraordinary *reductiones ad absurdum* of the replacement of nature with artifact as the focus of our sensory and mental attention, but examples of lesser severity would be easy enough to multiply. The net result, however, is that it is now possible to speak not only of addictions and social pathologies that most evidently and directly corrupt and distort the mind, but also of a new defect that has been labeled "nature deficit disorder."[45]

What needs to be done to help those who have lost or damaged their native attraction to the understated loveliness and intelligibility of nature, as Benedict XVI has counseled in a different but parallel

---

42. *Summa Theologiae* I-II, 53.3, Dominican Fathers translation.

43. Joseph Cardinal Ratzinger, "Consumer Materialism and Christian Hope," in Tom Horwood, ed., *Teachers of the Faith: Speeches and Lectures by Catholic Bishops* (London: Catholic Bishops' Conference of England and Wales, 2002), 81.

44. Reinhard Hütter, "Pornography and Acedia," *Nova et Vetera*, English edition 10 (2012): 901–7.

45. Richard Louv, *Last Child in the Woods: Saving our Children from Nature-Deficit Disorder* (New York: Workman, 2005), 33.

context, is for "the windows [to] be flung open again" so that they can "see the wide world, the sky and the earth once more."[46] And they must be helped to cultivate the practices that keep us from vagueness and that form our interior senses that they might serve rather than obstruct the understanding. These practices involve the use of the senses, but are essentially the work of the mind, for they are practices of looking and listening, of comparing things, of weighing characteristics with careful speech, and, especially, of looking before and after in order to place things in their appropriate genera and species and patiently discussing the natures of things and their definitions with our fellow inquirers. Although initially arduous, these practices not only bear lasting fruit, they also inculcate an habitual attentiveness that is a real perfection of the will and greatly prized by those who have learned to appreciate it. Gilbert Highet's praise for Louis Agassiz's pedagogical method in his *Art of Teaching* is one instance, but others can be readily supplied from our own experiences of sound and demanding courses of instruction.[47] Among the many contemporary pleas for the cultivation of attentiveness, few have been as eloquent as the one penned by the late historian of psychology Edward Reed: "Surely it is time," he observed, to "relearn the homely lesson that all understanding . . . is rooted in ordinary experience. The meaning of our lives will be found only when we make the effort to look for ourselves."[48] Perhaps, in this regard, it may be said that one of the aspects of Aristotle that still awaits recovery by Thomists is the attentiveness to being that is praised in the famous passage in *Parts of Animals* I.5 and embodied throughout his biological corpus.

---

46. Benedict XVI, "The Listening Heart: Reflections on the Foundations of Law," an address delivered in the Reichstag Building, Berlin, 22 September 2011.

47. See Gilbert Highet, *The Art of Teaching* (New York: Vintage, 1955), 214–17.

48. Edward S. Reed, *The Necessity of Experience* (New Haven: Yale University Press, 1996), 163.

Bearers of Wisdom

It is in Aquinas's first cause of restraint in the desire for knowledge that may be found an important teaching about the intellectual virtue of wisdom, that is, in the injunction that the student attend to the matters his state in life requires him to know. Two lessons seem to be implied by this injunction: first, that we ought to desire to climb to the heights of acquired wisdom just in so far as our state in life affords us a fitting opportunity to do so—no more and no less; second, that to whatever extent we have acquired wisdom, so also ought we to desire to share that wisdom by, as it were, coming back down from the heights, in order to make straight and smooth and as wide as possible the path that leads back to them. This twofold restraint is, on the one hand, a holding back from using our leisure to learn about trivial things and thus be distracted from the pursuit of wisdom, and, on the other, a refraining from a selfish enjoyment of whatever wisdom we have acquired that is shaped by a positive desire to teach those elementary studies and lower disciplines that enabled us to climb wisdom's slopes in the first place. The ordering to which the wise are called, on this view, involves a continual climbing up and returning back in order to assist others with their ascent.

It is a happy irony to be able to call upon a sophist to argue the point at hand. The late Richard Rorty, although no friend to wisdom, wonder, or truth, was as well acquainted with contemporary academic life as any. He once testified to his hope that "the students can be distracted from their struggle to get into a high-paying profession, and that the professors will not *simply* try to reproduce themselves by preparing the students to enter graduate study in their own disciplines."[49] His comment accurately points out the habits that are opposed to the

---

49. Richard Rorty, "Education as Socialization and as Individualization," [1989] in his *Philosophy and Social Hope* (London: Penguin, 1999), 116. Cf. Alasdair MacIntyre, "Catholic Universities: Dangers, Hopes, Choices," in *Higher Learning and Catholic Traditions*, ed. Robert E. Sullivan (Notre Dame: University of Notre Dame Press, 2001), 1–21, at 6: "The undergraduate major . . . becomes increasingly no more than a prologue to graduate school, even for those who will never go to graduate school."

studiousness that conduces to wisdom: the bad habit of the student who fails to gird his loins for the ascent (and such a student may very well be a teacher by profession), and the still worse habit of the teacher who has lost sight of his proper task and its true ordination to the common good. The first vice is easy to understand, widespread, and as old as Meno and Thrasymachus; its prevalence explains why some theories of intellectual virtue are content to affirm a strong desire for "epistemic goods" as a sufficient account of a healthy mental life: at least there *is* a mental life in such a case. The second vice is one that we tradesmen best understand, for in our weaker moments we see it in ourselves. A long life in the cabinetmaker's shop tends to make the back stoop and the eyes see every tree as only a bed or a dresser waiting to happen, and something similar happens to us scholars. We need not look abroad to understand the force of MacIntyre's observation that "there has developed since [Hume] a kind of philosophy that sometimes functions for those who engage in it just as dining and backgammon did for Hume."[50] MacIntyre himself has provided a suitable statement of the criterion by which we may assess the rectitude of our own habit of desiring knowledge. "Being a great philosopher," he suggests, "is not at all the same thing as leading an exemplary philosophical life, but perhaps the point of doing philosophy is to enable people to lead, so far as it is within their power, philosophical lives."[51]

In pursuit of the call to be truly studious by ardently desiring to realize the maxim *sapientis est ordinare* in all of its amplitude we have been given an exemplar and guide in Benedict XVI. He has developed a beautiful teaching about a virtue he calls intellectual charity. By this phrase he does not mean that every text ought to be read with the same sympathy and docility that we give to the works of the Fathers of the Church. Nor does he mean that we ought not argue, and strenuously if need be, for the truth of the faith. Quite the contrary. "This aspect of charity," he explains, "calls the educator to recognize that

---

50. MacIntyre, "The Ends of Life, The Ends of Philosophical Writing," in his *The Tasks of Philosophy*, 132.

51. Ibid, 132.

the profound responsibility to lead the young to truth is nothing less than an act of love." In practice, he notes, the work of this virtue is to "uphold the essential unity of knowledge against the fragmentation which ensues when reason is detached from the pursuit of truth" and "guide the young towards the deep satisfaction of exercising freedom in relation to truth."[52] Perhaps it is because he stands to the whole world as an elder that he understood his own Petrine ministry as an exercise of intellectual charity, making his own the "task to safeguard sensibility to the truth; to invite reason to set out ever anew in search of what is true and good, in search of God."[53]

To the extent to which we are narrowly immersed in a research agenda, have allowed our mind to be shaped by human conventions rather than to be measured by the being of things created by God, and finally, have not labored in the elementary studies that students must master if they are to make genuine progress in knowing and toward wisdom, to that same degree will we be unlikely to perceive in Aquinas's conception of studiousness a wise restraint by which the desire for knowledge is ordered to the attainment of the intellectual virtues. Instead, the practices that characterize studiousness may well seem to us as so much timidity in the face of knowledge-making. Those "bearers of wisdom" who have tasted something of the fruitfulness of restraint, however, are not likely to agree.[54]

---

52. Benedict XVI, Address to Educators, Washington, DC, 17 April 2008. See also the encyclical *Caritas in Veritate*, §1-6 (2009), his Homily for First Vespers with University Students of Rome, 17 December 2009, and "Saint Augustine of Hippo (4)," General Audience Address of 20 February 2008.

53. Benedict XVI, Address at La Sapienza, the University of Rome, 17 January 2008.

54. Benedict XVI, Address to Catholic Educators, Washington, DC, 17 April 2008.

4

The Recovery of Experience

"TO DEFEND THE TRUTH, to articulate it with humility and conviction, and to bear witness to it in life are," in the words of Benedict XVI, "exacting and indispensable forms of charity."[1] Truth is a universal good; prudently and dispassionately to bring the light of truth into human affairs always serves the cause of humanity, especially where truth is most fragmented or veiled. A Christian looking upon the many paradoxes of contemporary environmentalism can hardly fail to see the movement's need for the careful analysis of principles, the far-seeing weighing of consequences, and precise, non-ideological speech. The Pope's discussion of the environment in *Caritas in Veritate* was, therefore, an instantiation of the very intellectual charity he called for. Environmentalism, much like contemporary economic and political life, does indeed seem likely to benefit from a dose of papal reasonableness. Yet Benedict XVI did more than merely correct; in *Caritas in Veritate* he also praised certain contemporary economic and political initiatives, even secular ones. Following his example, we would do well to ask what contemporary environmentalism might have to offer to our common pursuit of the good of "the whole man and [of] every man."[2] One of the most salutary features of contem-

---

1. Benedict XVI, *Caritas in Veritate*, §1, Vatican translation.
2. See *Caritas in Veritate*, §18: "The truth of development consists in its completeness: if it does not involve the whole man and every man, it is not true development."

porary environmentalism is its concern that our generation recover first-hand experience of nature. If the search for a Christian environmentalism were to lead to a genuine recovery of experience, not only would a deeper and more widespread gratitude for the Creation likely result, but we could also discover fruitful soil for the renewal of Catholic philosophy envisioned and called for by St. John Paul II and Benedict XVI.

Beginning in Experience

Many environmentalists are also devoted students of nature; most naturalists, it seems, are also environmentalists, at least with some degree of commitment. Such a coincidence can hardly be accidental. We can only love what we know, and we tend to study what we love. In his popular ecological primer, *Reading the Forested Landscape*, Tom Wessels suggests that learning to perceive the essential structural features of a stand of trees can help to bring about a change in sentiment: "This new way of seeing creates reverence, respect, a sense of inclusion, and accountability. Reading the landscape is not just about identifying landscape patterns; more importantly, it is an interactive narrative that involves humans and nature."[3] The ability to perceive and to understand the effects of disturbance upon a forest, gained by repeated walks in the woods, promotes a sense of responsibility for the land. If experience shapes our desires, it just as plainly shapes knowledge and skill. In an essay published several years ago in the *American Naturalist*, marine ecologist Paul Dayton warned that even should the desire to conserve the environment be present, the knowledge of how to do so will not unless our ecologists and conservationists gain more extensive first-hand experience of nature. "Very few students," he lamented, "are offered the opportunity of observing nature and accumulating the background natural history essential to the ecological understanding" that the task of conservation requires. His point

---

3. Tom Wessels, *Reading the Forested Landscape: A Natural History of New England* (Woodstock, VT: Countryman Press, 1997), 21.

is worth underscoring. Practicing ecologists admit that the work of "knowledgeable local" biologists exercising "sound judgment" about the ecological communities they study is indispensable for any useful or trustworthy assessment of the healthy structure and function of a given ecosystem.[4] Dayton's universal conclusion is, then, well-stated: "We cannot protect or restore what we do not know."[5]

Is the first-hand experience of nature now something rare? Such is the claim of Richard Louv's much talked-about book, *Last Child in the Woods*. In his wide-ranging and ambitious essay, Louv points out the dangers of what he thinks to be so common a condition as to merit the clinical name of "nature-deficit disorder." By this phrase he means "the human costs of alienation from nature" such as the "diminished use of the senses, attention difficulties, and higher rates of physical and emotional illnesses."[6] Thanks, he posits, chiefly to the progressive urbanization of our society (less than 2 percent of the American population now lives on farms), to a habit of an immoderate use of television, and to the spread of air-conditioning, children growing up today are likely to be appallingly ignorant of the most basic natural phenomena and, what is more, utterly carefree in their ignorance. Louv cites a recent British study showing "that the average eight-year-old was better able to identify characters from the Japanese card trading game Pokemon than native species in the community where they lived: Pikachu, Metapod, and Wigglytuff were names more familiar to them than otter, beetle, and oak tree."[7] Alarmed by the near-total victory of computer games over the activities that were the source of his childhood delights—especially building tree houses and romping through the woods—and fearing that "as the care for nature increasingly becomes an intellectual concept severed from the joyful experi-

---

4. James R. Karr, "Assessment of Biotic Integrity Using Fish Communities," *Fisheries* 6 (1981): 21–27.

5. Paul K. Dayton, "The Importance of the Natural Sciences to Conservation," *The American Naturalist* 162 (2003): 12.

6. Richard Louv, *Last Child in the Woods: Saving Our Children from Nature-Deficit Disorder* (New York: Workman, 2005), 34.

7. Ibid., 33.

ence of the outdoors," he asks with some urgency, "Where will the future environmentalists come from?"[8] Like the ecologists Wessels and Dayton, he sees the remedy in a renewed cultivation of the first-hand experience of nature.

A recovery of the experience of nature, however, will only come about as the result of a determined effort, for, as Edward S. Reed has argued, both our shared habits of mind and our common way of life have made meaningful first-hand experience something rare and difficult to attain. In his 1996 essay *The Necessity of Experience*, Reed criticized the notion that the emerging information-based economy would pay dividends in happier workers more able to employ their creative talents and to thrive in worker-centered environments. Our reigning management styles and doctrines, he argued, would ensure that most would instead be "doomed to spend much of [their] work time . . . pushing buttons, dragging light beams, and responding like machines to symbols created by someone else."[9] Nor did he think us more likely to experience reality at home, for there we tend to encounter the world not directly, but through various media. "Now people look at television," Reed observed, "they no longer look at things for themselves." The danger of this habit stems not only from the fact that the information is selected for us, but also that it is increasingly presented to us in the form of what he called a "multilevel montage" in which a variety of sounds and images are spliced and re-presented in ways in which they never could be by nature. This technique, he allowed, "makes for fast-moving, snappy commercials and music videos," and, we might add, flashy websites, but it also "by definition replaces the causal structure of real experience with narrative structure(s) and voice(s)."[10] In other words, both at work and at play, we are continually presented with second-hand information and pre-packaged perception. Such a condition, on Reed's account, is an eerie *reductio ad absurdam* of the tendency

---

8. Ibid., 145–46.

9. Edward S. Reed, *The Neccesity of Experience* (New Haven: Yale University Press, 1996), 1.

10. Ibid., 108, 110–11.

common to modern philosophy to degrade or even to reject primary experience as naive and pre-critical.[11] And even if most Catholic philosophers defend the reliability of our sense impressions—and thus our experience of the world—in one way or another, these are defenses against arguments, not attempts to adjust and to correct widely shared and deeply ingrained habits. If Reed, Louv, and the naturalists are correct, however, our divorce from the world is a problem in urgent need of practical remedies.

Common to these arguments in favor of experience is that they dwell upon the consequences of our loss of it, consequences as diverse as psychological disorder, the loss of understanding, and changes in desire. This common feature should not be a cause of surprise. It is hardly possible to vindicate the necessity of sense experience by an appeal to some prior principle; how, after all, would such a principle come to be known if not through experience? What can be added to their diagnosis, however, is an attempt to identify the kind of experience they seek to recover and to explain its salient features. The kind of person who enjoys the experience promoted by the environmentalists seems plain enough: it is the student of nature, the naturalist. But what kind of experience of nature does the naturalist enjoy? In order to sketch an answer, we can do no better than to attend to the example and the writings of the first of naturalists, Aristotle.

Pied Beauty

Born to a physician's family, Aristotle took a keen interest in living things and their bodies, and, what is more, he paid close attention to the more extensive and specialized experience of those who were entirely devoted to some aspect of nature. Physicians, accordingly, do not figure in his works only as examples of artisans, but also as authorities in their own right, at least, that is, when they are what he called the "more philosophical kind" of physicians. Even fishermen

---

11. See Reed, 10–18.

were to him a source of knowledge about nature.[12] As to Aristotle's own field work, no less a naturalist than Darwin called him "one of the greatest, if not the greatest, observers that ever lived."[13] It is a commonplace among scholars that Aristotle's biological studies lay at the origin of his view of substance and of his confidence that the universal names that we predicate of individual living things are less the products of human willfulness than they are signs of constraints imposed by "truth itself."[14] "Aristotle, as much as any naturalist," wrote G. E. R. Lloyd, "appreciated that while it is the individual specimen that the biologist investigates, he does so from the point of view of the species as a whole and of what is common to all or most of its members, not from the point of view of the peculiarities of the individual specimen itself."[15] In a similar vein, Marjorie Grene asked why we should "take all this trouble with the arid texts of Aristotle?" Precisely because Aristotle was a biologist, and "biology can teach us better and more directly than the exact sciences the all-important role of pattern in the world and of comprehension in our knowledge of it."[16] Both comments point to the essential contours of the naturalist's way of knowing: he first distinguishes the differences among individual things, and then perceives the patterns that rise above the differences.

Let us consider how a young naturalist might come to learn about the woods near his home. The first impressions, of course, are

---

12. On the physicians who "study their art more philosophically," see *Sense and Sensibilia*, 1.436a20 and also *On Youth, Old Age, Life and Death, and Respiration*, 27(21).480b26ff. Fishing and fishermen appear, *inter alia*, in *History of Animals*, VIII.2 and VIII.19 and IX.37. All quotations of the works of Aristotle are taken from Jonathan Barnes, ed., *The Complete Works of Aristotle: The Revised Oxford Translation*, 2 volumes (Princeton: Princeton University Press, 1984).

13. In a letter of 1879, quoted in Gertrude Himmelfarb, *Darwin and the Darwinian Revolution* (New York: Norton, 1959), 169.

14. I am borrowing a phrase used by Aristotle with respect to his conclusion that the principles of nature must be contraries. See *Physics*, 1.5.188b30.

15. G. E. R. Lloyd, *Aristotle: The Growth and Structure of his Thought* (Cambridge: Cambridge University Press, 1968), 91–92.

16. Marjorie Grene, *A Portrait of Aristotle* (Chicago: University of Chicago Press, 1963), 229.

vague: the woods are dark compared to the grassy yard. The trees are tall, with brown trunks and green leaves. Soon, however, attention is repaid with the awareness of differences. Some trees have needles, others have leaves. Of those with leaves, some are compound, others simple; some have leaves in pairs on opposite sides of the branches, others have leaves that alternate, first on one side of the branch, then on the other. The needle-bearing trees sometimes have needles arranged singly on the branch, sometimes in bundles of two, three, or even five needles each. With the help of some additional study and a guidebook or two, the student is soon able to perceive that common features bind together different trees in spite of marked differences among individuals. A young black cherry growing on the edge of a field looks very different from an older one growing amidst the forest; a pitch pine on deep, moist soil almost looks like its aristocratic cousin the white pine, but on a dry, rocky, south-facing slope reverts to its normal, misshapen self. To the beginner, this wide variation between individuals causes confusion, but as more time is spent comparing individuals, the common nature becomes perceptible. This comparison is, as Aquinas notes, a "kind of reasoning," for what is required of the naturalist is to interrogate his senses by repeatedly asking himself to attend to the differences they reveal: are the lobes of the leaf tipped in spines or rounded? Are the lobes deeply or shallowly incised? Is the leaf smooth or velvety? Is the tree growing in a wet area or a dry one?[17] Eventually, from the forest and its welter of differences, the kinds of trees begin to stand out and to be recognized for what they are, and being known, they are named.[18] As his wanderings in the woods continue, the naturalist is

---

17. St. Thomas Aquinas, *Commentary on Aristotle's* Posterior Analytics, Book II, Lectio 19, trans. Richard Berquist (South Bend, IN: Dumb Ox Books, 2007), 339. "Experience requires a kind of reasoning about particulars, a reasoning that compares one thing to another." On the interplay between the perception of difference and sameness in coming to know, see Robert Sokolowski, "The Method of Philosophy: Making Distinctions," *Review of Metaphysics* 51 (1998): 515–32.

18. Compare *Summa Theologiae* I, Q. 94, Art. 3, sed contra: "Nomina autem debent naturis rerum congruere."

able to see patterns in the distribution of these kinds: the hemlocks and red maples are often found near stream beds or in wet soils, the hickories and white oaks on the dry hillsides; here is a pure stand of sugar maple, there is a mixed stand of red and white oaks, sugar maple, and hickory, with paper birch, red maple, and white pine on the margins. These patterns both shed further light upon the specific characteristics of the trees and also prompt the naturalist to wonder about their causes.

In all of this wondering and wandering, the naturalist's attention is taken up by the trees themselves, which he contemplates in the condition in which they are found, as independently existing individuals. Here lies the most striking difference between the practice of the naturalist or natural historian and of the contemporary scientist, who analyzes from the outset. Thus Theophrastus, Aristotle's successor at the Lyceum, argued that the study of plants ought to begin with the consideration of the tree, for the tree is a complete plant, in addition to being the easiest to study because the longest-lived and the largest.[19] Today's typical botany textbook, by comparison, begins with the cell, which though doubtless worthy of attention, is hardly first in our experience.[20] Aristotle, likewise, considers animals as integral wholes and compares them to one another "in their modes of subsistence, in their actions, in their habits, and in their parts;" even his consideration of the differing parts of animals is made in view of how the whole animals relate to one another and how the different kinds of animal bodies relate to the human body.[21] This emphasis on understanding the individual living thing as an integral whole accords well with the moral impulse of contemporary environmentalism. Although in some quarters attempts are being made to redefine the concept of biodiversity in the broadest possible terms, we are not likely to see many

---

19. See Theophrastus, *Enquiry into Plants* [1.1.11], 2 volumes, trans. Sir Arthur Hort, *Loeb Classical Library* (London: Heinemann, 1956), I:15.

20. See "The Plant Cell," which is the first section of Peter H. Raven, Ray F. Evert, and Susan E. Eichhorn, *Biology of Plants*, 4th edition (New York: Worth Publishing, 1986), 13–67.

21. Quotation from *History of Animals*, 1.1.487a11–14. And see *HA*, 1.6.491a14–22.

placards calling for us to "Save the Viruses." Bluebirds, dolphins, and orchids motivate environmentalists because they can be seen and appreciated as growing, living, and reproducing beings. Birdhouses are built and starlings and sparrows are evicted from them because conservationists are able to recognize the goodness of bluebirds, a goodness sufficiently plain to trump the claims of pluralism. Environmentalists fight for the lives of these creatures because they have seen them and beheld their beauty.

In their considering and beholding, naturalists develop a certain virtue that is worthy of wide imitation. Nature, as the sage put it, "loves to hide," and anyone who has spent some time in birdwatching knows the truth of that saying.[22] A firm disposition to attend to nature must be acquired if one is to learn about living things. Not only must one brave inclement weather, wet feet, and bug bites, but, most importantly, the naturalist must learn to be still and quiet. It may be thanks in part to his field experience that Aristotle said that "the possession of understanding and knowledge is produced by the soul's settling down out of the restlessness natural to it."[23] A trip into the field with a naturalist in early autumn may help to show how this is so. Our first impressions are of the colors: blaze-red maples against a backdrop of green pines and a light blue sky. There are no birds to be seen, so the naturalist bids us to listen. At first, there is nothing but road noise to be heard. Then harsh caws and jays stand out, and, in the distance, the honking of geese. As we settle down further and attend more carefully, other sounds emerge: the liquid note of a robin from atop a pine; a persistent chip followed by a flash of red through the alders—a cardinal; an odd, almost frog-sounding *mawk, mawk* from a tree trunk, and from the same tree, "dee-dee-dee"—the nuthatch and the chickadee. A few moments later we hear the rhythmic per-chick-o-ree of a goldfinch flying overhead followed by the mewing of the last catbird to linger in the North. Such are the sounds of a modest, but

---

22. Heraclitus, quoted in Jonathan Barnes, *Early Greek Philosophy*, 2nd edition (London: Penguin), 68.

23. *Physics* 7.3.247b18–20.

good trip into the field: the students heard and saw what the naturalist expected and were able to profit from his ability to direct their senses. The excellence that the naturalist-teacher has attained through practice, is in turn handed on to his students; it is an excellence of the use of the senses, an attentiveness that seems to make his hearing more acute and his eyesight more sharp, because he has learned how to watch and to listen.[24]

This attentiveness is not merely a physical skill like the ability to ride a bicycle, it is also an intellectual disposition that manifests itself in studious practices. Here the example of John James Audubon is instructive. In the introduction to the final volume of his *Ornithological Biography*, Audubon gave his readers a piece of advice. Expecting them to be "full of ardor" to learn about birds, he counseled them to "leave nothing to memory." "Note down all our observations," he said, and "with ink, not with black-lead pencil; and keep in mind that the more particulars you write at the time, the more you will afterwards recollect."[25] It is surely a home truth that the eye, like the mind, tends to wander. Every parent knows the importance of insisting upon eye contact with errant children: if the message is to go home, the eyes must be met. Audubon's practice reveals a similar homespun wisdom. Who has not sat on a stone wall or bench and enjoyed a distant view of a mountain or a sunset or a shoreline? In mere seconds the mind is dulled by the loveliness of the scene and the eyes, in concert with dreamy sentiment, begin to glaze over. Only the vaguest impressions are likely to remain because, in fact, few details were seen. As if to guard against this tendency, Audubon habitually focused his mind and his eyes by taking notes and by sketching, and so do all serious naturalists. By cultivating such a habit of observation, we can come to employ our senses more attentively, and perhaps even, as Josef Pieper

---

24. Compare Aquinas's "On the Teacher," in Ralph McInerny, ed. and trans., Thomas Aquinas, *Selected Writings* (London: Penguin, 1998), 199: "the teacher leads another in the same way to knowledge of the unknown as one by discovery brings himself to knowledge of the unknown."

25. John James Audubon, *Ornithological Biography* [1839] in *The Audubon Reader*, ed. Richard Rhodes (New York: Knopf, 2006), 608–9.

so insistently recommended two generations ago, learn "how to see again."[26]

It is all to the good to have more detailed and memorable experiences of the natural world, but how, one might ask, do they contribute both to the grounding of an environmental ethic and to the renewal of philosophy? The answer is that genuine experience of nature gives rise to wonder. Like Thales marveling at the regularity of the heavens, the naturalist perceives patterns and order in nature and is prompted to ask the reason for the orderliness. Real wonder—and here the Latin *admiratio* may be more suggestive—implies a recognition of the beauty of the created order, an intelligible beauty that points to the possibility of fulfillment in knowledge. Aquinas maintains that wonder is "a cause of delight to the extent that it has joined to it a hope of attaining the knowledge of what one desires to know."[27] We do not admire random occurrences; we are frightened by them. Yet even a blizzard can be admired, though its power is feared, because it follows an intelligible course. If wonder is in the first place a "path towards the seeking of wisdom," it can also be "the deepest source of the moral impulse."[28] "Tell me what you admire," said the late Servais Pinckaers, "and I will tell who you are."[29] The naturalist, ever-attentive to differences, to "All things counter, original, spare, [and] strange," may occasionally catch a glimpse of the source, of the one "whose beauty is past change," and, if his spirit has not been entirely beaten down by the grim rhetoric of Darwinism, may be moved to "Praise him."[30] The movement

---

26. See Pieper, "Learning How to See Again," in *Only the Lover Sings* (San Francisco: Ignatius, 1990), 31–36.

27. *Summa Theologiae* I-II, Q. 32, Art. 8, corpus: "Et ideo admiratio est causa delectationis inquantum habet adiunctam spem consequendi cognitionem eius quod scire desiderat."

28. *Summa Theologiae* I-II, Q. 32, Art. 8. The second objection begins "admiratio est principium sapientiae, quasi via ad inquirendum veritatem."

29. Servais Pinckaers, O.P., *A l'école de l'admiration* (Paris: Editions St. Paul, 2001), 5. "L'admiration constitue, à notre avis, la source la plus profonde de l'énergie et de la qualité morales."

30. Gerard Manley Hopkins, "Pied Beauty," in Hopkins, *The Major Works*, ed. Catherine Phillips (New York: Oxford University Press, 2002), 132–33.

of the soul captured in the 104th Psalm is most natural to human beings in the presence of the wonders of nature. The contemporary environmentalist's love for "cedars of Lebanon" and "high mountains" with their "wild goats" is not so much lacking in gratitude, as it is in gratitude's proper object. The language employed by Benedict XVI in *Caritas in Veritate* ought therefore to be congenial to open-minded environmentalists, for it affirms the goodness of the earth: "The environment is God's gift . . . it is prior to us . . . it is a wondrous work . . . containing a 'grammar' which sets forth ends and criteria for wise use."[31] That grammar, we might add, may only be learned from the Creation itself; the fabrications of human theory, when imposed upon nature, all too often result in ugly wounds.

A grateful admiration of the beauty, intelligibility, and goodness of the Creation also holds much promise for the renewal of philosophy. That there is a moral disposition necessary for the attainment of truth was a common theme in pontificates of Pope St. John Paul II and Benedict XVI. Benedict XVI has told us that we need "courage" in order to "engage the whole breadth of reason;" and in order for our inquiries to be fruitful, they must be undertaken, John Paul II taught, "with mind and heart rightly tuned."[32] A revivified philosophy will, of course, take the form of sharper arguments, clearer propositions, and more expansive explanations, but it will not be brought about by love of argument alone. The love of argument makes us disputatious; it is the love of truth that enlivens the philosophical soul and inspires courageous study. Though we catch mere glimpses of it, this truth is written into the natures of things. Philosophy's daily work is indeed like a meaty fist thumping with an argument the Manichees cannot answer, but its birth is in gazing over hills and asking, "What is God?" If concern for the condition of the earth prompts the next generation of students more often to stare admiringly at the hills, and by attentive watching and listening to nourish their ability to wonder, then the cause of truth will have been well-served by environmentalism.

---

31. *Caritas in Veritate*, §48.
32. Benedict XVI, "Faith, Reason, and the University: Memories and Reflection," #62; John Paul II, *Fides et Ratio*, §48.

5

The Beauty of Reasoning

"WHAT AN EXERCISE IN logical precision it is," said Bl. John Henry Newman, "to understand and enunciate the proof of any of the more difficult propositions in Euclid."[1] Newman knew first-hand the value of Euclid's *Elements of Geometry*. When he first arrived at Oxford, in the fall of 1817, he found himself faced with a demanding mathematics tutor who quizzed him about his preparation. "I believe, Sir, you never saw Euclid before?" Newman replied that he had "been over five books," but added "I could not say I knew them *perfect* by any means." The skeptical tutor asked Newman "what a point was, and what a line, and what a plane angle," and upon the student's correct answers, told him that he should come "with the other gentlemen at 10 o'clock with the 4th, 5th, and 6th Books." "And today," Newman triumphantly told his mother, "after I had demonstrated a tough one out of the 5th Book, he told me I had done it very correctly." Indeed, he became so confident in his mastery of the material that when given a choice of texts on which to be examined at the end of the term, he picked "the 5th Book of Euclid, the hardest book of Euclid . . . the ratio of ratios book."[2] Newman was surely right to see Book V of Euclid's

---

1. John Henry Newman, "Discipline of Mind," in *The Idea of a University*, ed. Martin J. Svaglic (Notre Dame: University of Notre Dame Press, 1982), 378.
2. Newman's letter of November 13, 1817, to his mother, in *The Letters and Diaries of John Henry Newman*, ed. Ian Ker and Thomas Gornall, S.J., volume 1 (Oxford: Clarendon Press, 1978), 44–45.

Elements as a worthy challenge. The book treats the theory of ratio and proportion in the abstract, that is, apart from the geometrical figures that the first four books examine. And the abstraction poses serious barriers to the student's progress in understanding, because the intellectual custom of our age does not dispose us readily to appreciate the beauty of reasoning, which is the chief and almost the sole beauty of Book V.

Book V may be called the "hardest Book of Euclid" for a number of reasons. Some of the difficulties arise from the dispositions of the student. First, by leaving behind the triangles, parallelograms, and circles of the first four books, Book V marks an abrupt caesura in the unfolding narrative of the art of geometry. The student no longer has the satisfaction of seeing a step-wise and cumulative gain of knowledge in continuity from the initial definitions of Book I. This discontinuity is unsettling, and the unsettled student finds arduous study more trying. A second difficulty caused by the abstraction from figures is that the student's desire to learn may be sapped. There is a dryness to the theorems of Book V from which those of the previous books do not suffer, for if it were difficult to muster up interest in parallelograms or triangles, the bare lines of Book V that stand for any magnitude whatever will quite possibly present no cause for admiration whatsoever. The third difficulty concerns the change in the quality of study that is required of the student. Our inherited and intuitive knowledge of simple geometrical figures makes many students able to guess the crux of a theorem in the first four books. Not so in Book V. Cleverness must be checked at the door, for the theorems are simply too far removed from common experience to admit of solution by guesswork.

Two further difficulties are intrinsic to the subject matter of Book V. The first is its new terminology. Because the theorems consider the truths of ratio and proportion in abstraction from figures, they must use a language that applies equally to every kind of figure and even to the parts of figures. The terms introduced in Book V, accordingly, are general ones, and in the English language they sound very much alike one another: magnitude, multiple, equimultiple. This new terminology is uncompromising. To master Book V the student must even employ prepositions with care and precision: "to be a multiple *of*" signifies one thing and "to have a ratio *to*" another. The second and most essential challenge of Book V lies in the nature of the reasoning it involves, which is at once spare and complex. It is spare because the syllogism is unveiled in all of the grandeur of its lucidity; it is complex because the major premise of the most important syllogisms in Book V is its daunting 5th definition:

> Magnitudes are said to be *in the same ratio*, the 1st to the 2nd and the 3rd to the 4th, when, if any equimultiples whatever be taken of the 1st and 3rd, and any equimultiples whatever of the 2nd and 4th, the former equimultiples alike exceed, are alike equal to, or alike fall short of, the latter equimultiples respectively taken in corresponding order.[3]

The simplicity and fertility of this definition are not immediately apparent. Yet in his history of ancient geometry, Proclus credited Euclid with "systematizing many of the theorems of Eudoxus," the original author of the theory of ratio and proportion.[4] If Euclid's great achievement was to have brought order and clarity to geometry, then it is worth assuming that a definition such as this one is in fact optimal. Our object here is to come to see that this is so.[5]

In order to appreciate the beauty of the reasoning in Book V, we must first gain a general understanding of the science of ratio and proportion, then explore the 5th definition and its role in the demonstra-

---

3. All quotations from Euclid's *Elements* are from the standard translation by Sir Thomas Heath, from the second edition published by Cambridge University Press in 1926 and now widely accessible in the series The Great Books of the Western World as well as in editions from Dover Publications and Green Lion Press.

4. Proclus, *A Commentary on the First Book of Euclid's* Elements, trans. Glenn R. Morrow (Princeton: Princeton University Press, 1992), 56.

5. This chapter was shaped by the unpublished doctoral dissertation of Michael Augros, "An Examination of Euclid's Elements," Boston College, 1994, as well as the teaching and conversation of Anthony Andres.

tions of Book V, and, finally, inquire how Book V makes possible the investigation of ratio and proportion in geometrical figures.

Ratio and Proportion

The shift between Books IV and V of the *Elements* may be understood as a change from the study of equality to that of inequality. The shift is a shock to the student, for equality is what makes quantity intelligible to us, as when we measure something. We come to know the length of a table-top by discovering that it is equal to so many feet, and the quantity of foot is known to us both from long use and because it relates to our immediate experience of distance through walking. If two or more quantities were simply unequal, we could say little more than "this one is larger," or, at best, "this one is much larger," and a reasoned-out account of their differences would be unnecessary. Books V and VI of the *Elements*, accordingly, do not study unequal things as such, but unequal things that have certain relations of equality to one another, as in "this is twice that," which is to say "this one is equal to two of those." The subject of Books V and VI, then, is the kind of equality that is found among unequal things, the equality of ratios otherwise known as proportion.

The terms "ratio" and "proportion" will be more easily understood if we attend to Euclid's usage of them. "Ratio" is a carrying-over, through the Latin, of the Greek term *logos*, a rich word that generally means either "speech" or "reason." In the context of Books V and VI of the *Elements*, ratio means "the account of the relationship in respect of size between two magnitudes of the same kind." "Proportion" is our English term for Euclid's *analogia*, a noun formed from the adjective *analogos*, which literally means "upon an account" or "according to an account." Euclid says, with his customary concision, "let magnitudes which have the same ratio be called proportional." It may be helpful to think of proportional magnitudes as unequal magnitudes about whose size some account may be given more than simply to say that they are not equal.

An elementary understanding of proportion is gained during

childhood. About the age of three, children begin keenly to notice inequality, especially when being served certain kinds of foods. They express their discovery in complaints such as "Why does John have more ice cream than I do?" The answer, of course, is that John is older. To explain that John has more ice cream because he is older is to employ a proportion that sets unequal ages and unequal requirements for a healthy diet into a relation of equality, a sameness of ratio. A scant quarter-cup of ice cream, say, is an appropriate reward for a three-year-old who has eaten her broccoli, while half a cup suits a nine-year-old who has eaten his larger portion.

As we mature, we begin to reflect upon proportion in connection with questions of justice. Much like the three-year-old girl, men and women are initially inclined to interpret justice as a matter of strict equality. Consider the example of a high-school graduate wondering why her elder brother received a larger gift at his graduation from college than she did for finishing the twelfth grade. The appropriate answer reposes upon the truth that justice is not a matter of strict equality, but instead, as Aristotle explains, "a species of the proportionate."[6] The just, in his case, is a certain sameness of relation or ratio that sets the rewards of the two siblings in proportion to their merits. As college requires a more arduous course of study than high school, it is fitting for the brother to receive a proportionally larger gift. "The just, therefore, involves at least four terms; for the persons for whom it is in fact just are two, and the things in which it is manifested, the object distributed, are two."[7] In other words, the ratio of the merit of the first to the merit of the second is equal to the ratio of the first reward to the second reward.

As in the case of justice, so also in the study of geometrical figures: strict equality is understood before sameness of ratio. For instance, in Book I the equality of triangles is considered in three different theorems, commonly known as "side-angle-side" (I.4), "side-side-side" (I.8), and "angle-side-angle" (I.26). In each case, the theorem exam-

---

6. Aristotle, *Nicomachean Ethics*, 5.3.1131a30.

7. *Nicomachean Ethics*, 5.3.1131a18–21 (Oxford translation).

ines the conditions under which we may conclude that two triangles are equal in every way, that is, both in shape and size. Later, in Book VI, comes the consideration of triangles which have the same shape but differ in size, in theorem VI.4, in which it is demonstrated that "in equiangular triangles, the sides about the equal angles are proportional." The theorem is particularly satisfying because it accords with our expectations. We may very well guess that the sides of equiangular triangles are proportional and that the triangles are therefore similar. What VI.4 does for us is to render that similarity fully known, that is, both explicit and as the result of reasoning from secure starting-points. We are able to conclude with certainty that though the six lengths (the sides of the two triangles) are disparate, they can be understood in terms of the kind of equality that is sameness of ratio.

The science of proportion in Book VI extends and deepens the treatment of geometrical figures contained in the first four books of the *Elements*. Consider theorem VI.31: "In right-angled triangles, the figure on the side subtending the right angle is equal to the sum of the similar and similarly described figures on the sides containing the right angle." The resonance of this proposition to the Pythagorean Theorem (I.47) is apparent. This one states in general terms what I.47 had said specifically about squares. In both cases, what is being said is that the sides of right triangles have a particular kind of relationship among them, which is not one of equality, but instead of the equality of the figures constructed upon them. Proclus was so impressed by VI.31 that he saw it as an indication of Euclid's superiority to Pythagoras: "though I marvel at those who first noted the truth of this theorem (I.47), I admire more the author of the Elements, not only for the very lucid proof by which he made it fast, but also because in the sixth book he laid hold of a theorem even more general than this and secured it by irrefutable scientific arguments."[8]

A still more significant example of the beautiful truths revealed by the study of ratio and proportion is theorem VI.30: "To cut a given finite straight line in extreme and mean ratio." Line AB is cut at E in

---

8. Proclus, *Commentary*, trans. Morrow, 338.

such a way that BE:EA::EA:AB.[9] Along the way, the rectangular parallelogram CD is constructed so as to be equal to the square on AB; by subtraction, then, the square AE is shown to be equal to the rectangle AB, BE. This same result had earlier been achieved in II.11 by means of the Pythagorean Theorem. Here a more supple construction allows for a more economical path to the same result. In addition, the science of proportion provides a deeper, more complete understanding of what had earlier been learned about the same construction. For in II.11, it was shown that a line had been cut so as to make the square on one of the parts equal to the rectangle contained by the whole and the remaining part. The original line, however, was not plainly related to the two parts other than by being one of the sides of the rectangle. With VI.30, the fate of the original line is more clearly understood: it has been cut in extreme and mean ratio, that is, the smaller part stands to the larger part in the same ratio that the larger part stands to the whole. What this cut or section in turn signifies Euclid does not say, for to do so would have taken him beyond the boundaries of Book VI. Yet we can see that there is something grand at stake. For this cut or section is no ordinary part, it is in fact an incommensurable or irrational ratio called the Golden Ratio or Golden Section.

The Definition of Sameness of Ratio

Having seen that the science of ratio and proportion adds breadth and depth to the study of geometrical figures, we now turn to the principles of the science itself. As in each of the first four books of the *Elements*, Book V begins with definitions. It is the 5th definition that poses a problem. Why is it so complex? Why must equimultiples be examined in order to determine whether magnitudes are proportional? In Book VII, after all, the definition of proportion in numbers is much simpler: "Numbers are proportional when the 1st is the same multiple,

---

9. The notation of ratio and proportion, which commonly takes the form A:B::C:D, is to be read this way: "A stands to B in the same ratio that C stands to D," or, in a geometrical shorthand, "A is to B as C is to D."

or the same part, or the same parts of the 2nd that the 3rd is of the 4th."
Thanks to the facility with numbers we gain in grammar school, we
readily perceive proportion in them, as in the following examples:

4:2::8:4   The 1st is the same multiple of the 2nd that the 3rd if of
            the 4th.
2:4::6:12   The 1st is the same part of the 2nd that the 3rd is of the
            4th.
3:4::6:8   The 1st is the same parts of the 2nd that the 3rd is of the
            4th.

A number, as Euclid teaches, is a "multitude composed of units."
All numbers have the unit as a common part or measure. Euclid's definition of proportion, therefore, is applicable to every number. Geometrical figures, however, are made of continuous rather than discrete
quantity. There is no unit in continuous quantity, and it is possible for
two magnitudes to lack a common measure, to be incommensurable.
That the side and the diagonal of a square have no common measure
was known by the time of Plato.[10] It is because there are incommensurable magnitudes that a more general theory of ratio and proportion is
necessary, and, with it, the taking and comparing of equimultiples. To
our age, the notion of incommensurability has been lost, thanks to the
custom of dissolving numbers into integers that are mere place-hold-
ers for use in equations. The typical student today takes as unprob-
lematic both negative numbers and repeating decimals and is likely to
be mystified by Euclid's general theory of proportion as a result.

The 5th definition of Book V understands proportion in terms of
its proper effect. Proportion in geometrical figures or their parts cannot be immediately judged in terms of common parts or a common
measure. But even incommensurable magnitudes—provided they be
of the same kind, as line and line—are capable of exceeding one another, and this is why the 5th definition attends to the equality or in-

---

10. See Thomas Heath, *A History of Greek Mathematics, volume I: From Thales to Euclid*
    (1921; Mineola, NY: Dover, 1981), 154–57.

equality of equimultiples. Proportional magnitudes, then, are those whose equimultiples exceed, equal, or fall short of one another in the order set down in the 5th definition, that is, when equimultiples have been taken of the 1st and 3rd magnitudes and others of the 2nd and 4th, then the multiple of the 1st term is compared to that of the 2nd and the multiple of the 3rd term to that of the 4th. The investigation of the equimultiples discloses whether the original magnitudes are proportional. The 5th definition, then, involves a kind of reasoning from the effect back to the cause.

In coming to appreciate the 5th definition, it helps to consider the 7th definition of Book V in comparison. "When, of the equimultiples, the multiple of the 1st magnitude exceeds that of the 2nd, but the multiple of the 3rd does not exceed the multiple of the 4th, then the 1st is said to have a greater ratio to the 2nd than the 3rd has to the 4th." Here is an example of the 7th definition in use:

```
A ------------         E ------------------------
B ------               G ------------------
C --------             F ----------------
D ------               H ------------------
```

A, B, C, and D are the original magnitudes. E and F are equimultiples of the 1st and 3rd magnitudes, that is, of A and C; each is double the original magnitude. G and H are other, chance equimultiples of the 2nd and 4th magnitudes, that is, of B and D; they happen to be three times the original magnitudes. G and H are called equimultiples because they are the product of the original magnitudes taken the same number of times. They are called chance equimultiples not because they happen to be the *same* multiple, but because the number by which the original magnitudes were multiplied happened to be three. When we compare the equimultiples, we see that the multiple of the 1st magnitude, namely E, exceeds that of the 2nd, G, while that of the 3rd, F, falls short of that of the 4th, H. We conclude, therefore, that the ratio of A to B is greater than that of C to D (A:B > C:D). When we inspect the original magnitudes, we see that the conclusion fits with what appears to be the case.

What if the original magnitudes had been in the same ratio? Let us recall the wording of the 5th definition: "Magnitudes are said to be *in the same ratio*, the 1st to the 2nd and the 3rd to the 4th, when, if any equimultiples whatever be taken of the 1st and 3rd, and any equimultiples whatever of the 2nd and 4th, the former equimultiples alike exceed, are alike equal to, or alike fall short of, the latter equimultiples respectively taken in corresponding order." The following example differs markedly from the previous one.

```
L --------            Q -----------------------
M ------              R -----------------------
N ----                S ------------
O ---                 T ------------
```

We have taken equimultiples of the 1st and 3rd terms, by taking L and N each three times to generate Q and S. We have taken other equimultiples of the 2nd and 4th terms. R and T are each four times M and O. In this case, Q is equal to R while S is equal to T. It is plain that if L and N had each been taken four times instead of three, then Q would exceed R while S would exceed T. Or, again, if L and N had each been taken twice instead of three times, then Q would fall short of R and S would fall short of T. Only when the original magnitudes are in the same ratio will the equimultiples *always* behave in the proper fashion. If, however, the ratio of the 1st to the 2nd had been different—say, greater—than that of the 3rd to the 4th, then there would be some combination of equimultiples that would not behave according to the dictates of the 5th definition, as we saw in the case of the first example above.

Of the twenty-five theorems in Book V, only ten require the investigation of equimultiples. The first of these is V.4: "If a 1st magnitude have to a 2nd the same ratio as a 3rd to a 4th, any equimultiples whatever of the 1st and 3rd will also have the same ratio to any equimultiples whatever of the 2nd and 4th respectively, taken in corresponding order."

Like each of the first six propositions in Book V, this theorem examines a characteristic property of equimultiples. These six theorems provide the tools for the consideration of equimultiples in the later propositions that treat proportion itself. Let us consider V.4 in detail.

The demonstration begins by laying down the four original magnitudes, which by hypothesis are in the same ratio (A:B::C:D). Then equimultiples are taken of the 1st and 3rd terms, and others of the 2nd and 4th terms.

A --------   C ----------
B ----   D -----

E ----------------   F --------------------
G ------------   H ---------------

In this case, E and F are each double A and C respectively, while G and H are each triple B and D. E, F, G, and H are now to be considered in themselves. Do they stand in the same ratio to one another, that is, does E stand to G in the same ratio that F stands to H (E:G::F:H)? Upon inspection, it appears likely that they do, but the geometer seeks certitude, not mere likelihood. The only way to know whether they are indeed proportional is to investigate the equimultiples that are generated from them. The next step in the demonstration, therefore, is once again to take chance equimultiples of the 1st and 3rd terms, and others of the 2nd and 4th terms.

K -----------------------   L ----------------------------
M -----------------------   N -------------------------------

As it happens, K and L are each double E and F, while M and N are each triple G and H. We must consider K, L, M, and N now as equimultiples, that is, as magnitudes that either exceed, equal, or fall short of one another taken in corresponding order. We are faced with a question: Is it the case that when K exceeds M, L also exceeds N, and that K is equal to M, L is equal to N, and, finally, that when K falls short of M, L also falls short of N?

Such a question would seem to be difficult to answer definitively. How are we to know anything about the relative sizes of all the different possible equimultiples that may be generated from the magnitudes E, F, G, and H? What we do know, however, is that those magnitudes were themselves generated by the multiplication of magnitudes that were by hypothesis proportional. The next step in the demonstration, therefore, is to relate K, L, M, and N back to the original, proportional magnitudes A, B, C, and D. This task may be accomplished thanks to the preceding theorem, V.3. It is not our business here to prove that theorem; it is enough for us to see that our present problem is solved by the truth that it revealed: "If a 1st magnitude be the same multiple of a 2nd that a 3rd is of a 4th, and if equimultiples be taken of the 1st and 3rd, then also *ex aequali* the magnitudes taken will be equimultiples respectively, the one of the 2nd and the other of the 4th." *Ex aequali* means "from the equal thing;" the connotation is that we are able to conclude equality "from the equal thing" that lies between the two objects in question, as though we were saying, in the present case, "equal multiples of equal multiples are also equal multiples of the original magnitudes."

Returning to our example, we may now apply V.3 to our equimultiples. A 1st magnitude, E, is the same multiple of a 2nd, A, that a 3rd, F, is of a 4th, C, and 5th magnitude, K, is the same multiple of the 1st, E, that a sixth, L, is of the 3rd, F; therefore the 5th and 6th magnitudes are also equimultiples respectively of the 2nd and 4th. That is to say that K and L are equimultiples of A and C. And for the same reason, M and N are equimultiples of B and D.

Now that we have successfully identified K, L, M, and N as equimultiples of the original magnitudes, which we know to be proportional, we may invoke the 5th definition. K and L and equimultiples of A and C, while M and N are other equimultiples of B and D, but A:B::C:D, therefore the following relationships of equality and inequality necessarily follow:

When K > M, also L > N;
When K = M, also L = N; and,
When K < M, also L < N.

In the example above, K and L each fall short of M and N respectively.

Having discovered the relationships that obtain among the equimultiples K, L, M, and N, we may now look back to the magnitudes from which they were generated, E, F, G, and H. Our reasoning, again, follows the course of the 5th definition, but this time in reverse. Since it is the case that

When K > M, also L > N;
When K = M, also L = N; and,
When K < M, also L < N,

while K and L are equimultiples of E and F and M and N are other equimultiples of G and H, then it follows that the original magnitudes are in the same ratio, the 1st standing to the 2nd in the same ratio that the 3rd stands to the 4th, or E:F::G:H. We have now completed the demonstration, for we have shown, with the help of the 5th definition, that if a 1st magnitude have to a 2nd the same ratio as a 3rd to a 4th, any equimultiples whatever of the 1st and 3rd will also have the same ratio to any equimultiples whatever of the 2nd and 4th respectively, taken in corresponding order.

In order to dispel a possible point of confusion, we should note that the ratio of E:G (and so also of F:H) is not necessarily the same ratio as A:B (or C:D). We can appreciate this fact better if we supply numbers to the magnitudes that we used in our example above. Recall that E and F were each double A and C, while G and H were each triple B and D:

A = 8   B = 4   C = 10   D = 5
E = 16   G = 12   F = 20   H = 15

The ratio of A:B is 8:4, or 2:1, while that of E:G is 16:12, that is 4:3. When we inspect the magnitudes with the help of numbers, then, it is plain that A:B::C:D and also that E:F::G:H, but also that the two sets of four magnitudes are not necessary in the same ratio with one another.

Now that we have carefully followed the demonstration of a theorem reposing upon the definition of sameness of ratio, we should stop to consider the form of reasoning employed in the demonstration. The 5th definition, although itself complex and even cumbersome, is employed in the simplest of syllogisms, those of the first figure. The identity of the major term is plain: "in the same ratio," or, simply "proportional." The middle term, however, cannot be so neatly expressed, for it is the proper relationship of the equimultiples generated from the original magnitudes. In other words, the middle term is the whole latter half of the 5th definition. For convenience, we may express it as magnitudes that generate equimultiples with the proper characteristics. The minor term can be thought of in two ways. Taken as a particular, the minor term is simply "these four magnitudes." As a universal, the minor term will vary according to what is proposed in the given theorem. In the case of V.4, the minor term would be "the equimultiples of the 1st and 3rd and the 2nd and 4th terms, respectively, of magnitudes that are in the same ratio." The concluding syllogism of V.4, then, would read as follows, formulated universally:

I.   Magnitudes that generate equimultiples with the proper characteristics are proportional.

II.   Magnitudes that are the equimultiples of the 1st and 3rd and the 2nd and 4th terms respectively of magnitudes that are in the same ratio are magnitudes that generate equimultiples with the proper characteristics.

Conclusion: Magnitudes that are the equimultiples of the 1st and 3rd and the 2nd and 4th terms respectively of magnitudes that are in the same ratio are proportional.

Midway through V.4 it was necessary to employ the 5th definition in reverse, that is, to place the relations of the equimultiples as the major term, with "proportional" as the middle term:

I.	Proportional magnitudes are magnitudes that generate equimultiples with the proper characteristics.
II.	These magnitudes (in our example: A, B, C, and D) are proportional.
Conclusion:	These magnitudes are magnitudes that generate equimultiples with the proper characteristics (in our example: K > M, L > N; K = M, L = N; K < M, L < N).

The essential structure, then, of the reasoning of the crucial propositions in Book V is to move through first-figure syllogisms employing the 5th definition in the major premise.

The Achievement of Book V

Having gained a general sense of the science of ratio and proportion and having examined the kind of reasoning that undergirds it in the central theorems of Book V, it remains to be seen how Book V makes possible the study of ratio and proportion in geometrical figures in Books VI and X through XIII of the *Elements*.

Book VI begins with a proposition that is essentially the same in structure as the crucial theorems of Book V, in that VI.1 reposes upon Book V's 5th definition. VI.1 proves that the areas of triangles and parallelograms with the same height are to one another as their bases, and it proceeds by the investigation of the equimultiples of the bases and the triangles. What VI.1 adds to the ordinary structure of the theorems that employ the 5th definition is the geometrical principle that triangles on equal bases and within the same parallels are equal in area (I.38). This truth secures the proper relation of the equimultiples, namely, when the multiple of the 1st base exceeds that of the 2nd, then the multiple of the 1st triangle will also exceed that of the 2nd, and if the bases are equal, the triangles will be as well, and if less, then less. As the entire subject of Book VI rests upon this theorem as its foundation, it is evident that Book VI also reposes upon the 5th definition and the form of reasoning that it requires.

A second way of perceiving the necessity of Book V for the science of ratio and proportion in geometrical figures is to examine the use of its theorems in the demonstrations of Book VI. What such an inquiry reveals is that five of the theorems of Book V are particularly important: V.7 together with its converse V.9, V.11, V.16, and V.22. Of these, the most frequently employed is V.11: "ratios which are the same with the same ratio are the same with one another." V.11 is directly used in eleven of the thirty-three theorems in Book VI. Also significant is V.24, which in effect allows the addition of proportions: if A:B::C:D and E:B::F:D, then A+E:B::C+F:D. Although V.24 is used only once in Book VI, the theorem in which it is used is the generalized restatement of the Pythagorean Theorem (VI.31) which, as we have seen, is one of the book's crowning achievements.

The most compelling witness to the importance of Book V is to be gained by considering its relation to the most significant theorem of Book VI, the cutting of a line in extreme and mean ratio (VI.30). This is that Golden Section so wonderfully employed in such buildings as the Parthenon and the Cathedral of Amiens and also in the form of the human body itself. What is more, the Golden Section is the linchpin that holds together the narrative structure of Euclid's *Elements*. As Proclus noted, Euclid, as a follower of Plato, conceived of "the goal of the *Elements* as a whole to be the construction of the so-called Platonic figures," those five solids made of equiangular and equilateral plane figures and inscribed in spheres: the pyramid, the square, the octagon, the icosahedron, and the dodecagon.[11] To create the last two of these figures, the twenty-sided and the twelve-sided, requires the ability to cut a line in extreme and mean ratio as well as the knowledge of the relations among the figures that may be generated from the parts of a

---

11. Proclus, *Commentary*, trans. Morrow, 57.

line so cut. The importance of VI.30 to the whole of Euclid's *Elements*, then, can scarcely be exaggerated. It is as good a candidate as any for the honor of most worthy theorem in the entire treatise. VI.30 is also a reliable gauge of the mastery of the first six Books of the *Elements*, for to be able to complete VI.30 requires not only the knowledge of the greater part of Book VI, but also of 18 of the 25 theorems contained in Book V.

As founding rector of the Catholic University of Ireland, John Henry Newman's essential task was to create an educational institution that would both be faithful to the Catholic intellectual tradition and well-suited to serve the needs of its constituents. It has perhaps not been sufficiently noted that in the works that he wrote to explain his choices, Newman not only defended the role of theology in education, but also fought the tendency of educators in his age to abandon those elementary studies, such as geometry, that he thought necessary for attaining discipline of mind. Indeed, he insisted that liberal education ought to be a training in reasoning and accuracy of thought, and he repeatedly warned of the tendency among the youth toward a "mental restlessness and curiosity" which was commonly joined to a distaste for mathematics. This disinclination he viewed in a sharply negative light: "it only means that they do not like application, they do not like attention, they shrink from the effort and labor of thinking, and the process of true intellectual gymnastics."[12] Yet Newman's educational vision was no mere posture of traditionalism. He held a compelling positive ideal, the "perfection of the Intellect" that resulted from the arduous training and careful course of study that he recommended. For the mind disciplined by liberal education, he explained, attains a "clear, calm, accurate vision and comprehension of all things," and "has almost the beauty and harmony of heavenly contemplation, so intimate is it with the eternal order of things and the music of the

---

12. Newman, "Elementary Studies," in *The Idea of a University*, 255–56.

spheres."[13] How fitting that Newman should have concluded his description of the educated mind on this Pythagorean note. His own mind had been formed not only by the Latin and Greek classics and the works of Aristotle, but also by Euclid's *Elements of Geometry*. At the heart of that great book, in the theory of ratio and proportion of Book V, one may indeed catch a glimpse of the beauty of reasoning.

---

13. *The Idea of a University*, 105.

6

Artisans of the Word

"IN THE BEGINNING WAS the Word." So Benedict XVI wrote on the pages of the Golden Book of the *Institut de France* during his visit to Paris in September 2008.[1] His choice of inscriptions is an occasion for wonder. The Pope's journey to France commemorated the Blessed Virgin Mary's appearances at Lourdes a century and a half before, but was also undertaken in service of the re-evangelization of Europe. To Europe, in a special way, the Word is indeed primary. As Benedict XVI affirmed at his speech at the *Collège des Bernadins* on the day before his visit to the *Institut*, the very "roots of European culture" are to be found in the reverence for the Word of God that was nourished in countless abbeys and convents during what might be called—following Newman—the "Benedictine period" of the history of Europe.[2] The men and women who, like St. Benedict, fled a world left in ruins by Rome's fall, did not do so "to create a culture nor even to preserve a culture from the past." No, the Pope insists, "they wanted to do the essential—to make an effort to find what was perennially valid and

---

1. See www.institut-de-france.fr/minisite/visite_pape /1211_signature_du_ livre_d_or.html.

2. See Newman's two essays "The Mission of St. Benedict" and "Benedictine Schools," in *Rise and Progress of Universities and Benedictine Essays*, with an introduction and notes by Mary Katherine Tillman (Notre Dame: University of Notre Dame Press, 2001), 365–487; the passage referred to is in "Benedictine Schools," at 486.

lasting, life itself. They were searching for God." Yet theirs was no unguided search into a "trackless wilderness," for "God himself had provided signposts" in "his word, which had been disclosed to men in the books of the sacred Scriptures." It is, therefore, by a certain "inner necessity," he explains, that "the search for God demands a culture of the word," that is to say, a set of practices and habits that enable believers better to hear and to understand, to meditate upon and to converse with, and to perform the Word of God.[3] Benedict XVI's inscription is an invitation to join him in the labor of rebuilding a culture of the word.

"In the beginning was the Word." Benedict XVI's choice of this passage as an epigraph in the home of the *Académie Française* is a reminder that the intellectual life is less complicated than it is sometimes thought to be. "All men by nature desire to know," said Aristotle.[4] At its deepest, this desire is a longing to know God. Yet God has spoken to us, "of old to our fathers by the prophets; but in these last days . . . by a Son" (Hebrews I.1). And so, adequately to fulfill our deepest desire for knowledge, we need chiefly to learn to hear the Word, to enter into conversation with the Word, and to perform the Word in imitation of Christ. These are the great tasks of the Christian life; they are also the labors that will rebuild a culture of the word. Benedict XVI's phrase "culture of the word" invites us to ask how the arts practiced by students and writers can contribute to the task of evangelization. In looking for an answer, sure resources are available in the lives and works of three great Christian writers, true artisans of the word. From the novelist, Jane Austen, we can learn of the kind of listening or hearing that a culture of the word requires as its first foundation. In the lyric poet Jean de la Cèppede we can find a model of meditating upon and conversing with the word. Finally, for a les-

---

3. Address of His Holiness Benedict XVI to Representatives from the World of Culture, Collège des Bernadins, Paris, France; 12 September 2008. Unless otherwise noted, all papal texts and discourses are quoted from the Vatican translations made available at www.vatican.va.

4. Aristotle, *Metaphysics*, 1.1

son in performance, we could do worse than to attend to perhaps the greatest artisan of the word ever to belong to the *Académie Française*, the poet and playwright Jean Racine.

Attending to the Word

"Listen, my son, to the master's instructions and take them to heart." So opens the handbook of the culture of the word, the *Rule of St. Benedict*. In the "school for the Lord's service" that is the monastery, "it is right that the master should speak and teach, while the disciple should be silent and listen." The silence required of the monastery's inhabitants may be the most imposing of the "tools for the spiritual craft," but it is also the most essential, for it is in the silence of contemplative prayer that Christ, the master, may be heard.[5] The one who chooses a life characterized by long periods of silence must have first tasted something of the consolation that prayer can bring. For those living amidst the hurly-burly of the world and the noisiness of daily life, silence is like a fine wine: its savor is all the more appreciated for being rarely sensed. To the harried parent of a large family, silence may almost seem like a refuge desirable in itself and for itself. Yet silence, like every other ascetic practice, derives its meaning from the end it is meant to serve, in this case the end of attentive listening and understanding. To this end, Jane Austen, a master of both listening and understanding, can help us to perceive the path.

It should be comforting to look to Jane Austen for a model of attentiveness, for she became an accomplished listener in spite of growing up in a noisy home. As if five older brothers were not enough (and she also had a younger one, as well as a sister), the Austen household also included—at various times—boarding students, visiting cousins, two horses, a milk cow, and a flock of chickens. Her brothers loved to act and to dance, so impromptu theatricals and balls like those described in *Mansfield Park* and *Persuasion* were part of the ordinary course of life. And there was plenty of conversation. "It was a cheer-

---

5. *Rule of St. Benedict*, trans. Carolinne White (London: Penguin, 2008), 7, 9, 21, 18.

ful house," according to her niece—who was old enough to recall it during one of its latter seasons—where the "family talk had much of spirit and vivacity."[6] Aunt Jane more than did her part in the noise-making. One of her nieces, wishing to give a rounded appreciation of her character, testified that "when grave she was very grave;" most times, however, "her unusually quick sense of the ridiculous inclined her to play with the trifling commonplaces of everyday life."[7] Another niece concurred, speaking of her "charm to children," the "delight of her playful talk," and her "most delightful stories chiefly of Fairyland." "*Every*thing she could make amusing to a child."[8] Upon hearing the same niece say that "she always encouraged my youthful belief in Mary Stuart's perfect innocence of all the crimes with which History has charged her memory," we may wish to conclude that even Aunt Jane's more serious moments were likely to be lively and tinged with romance.[9] Few novelists have done as much as Jane Austen to support Cicero's suggestion that nothing is "more pleasant or more properly human than to be able to engage in elegant conversation."[10] From the searching tête-à-tête of Anne Elliot discussing the choice of books with Captain Benwick to the sparkling repartee of Eliza Bennet's talk while dancing with Mr. Darcy at Netherfield, conversations in Jane Austen's novels can show their characters at their most attractive.

With all this talk, where is the room for listening? The answer is not far afield: if another is speaking, then one's duty and privilege is to listen. In an age in which the television has replaced the hearth, it may be difficult for us to appreciate the possibility of listening to others

---

6. Caroline Austen, "My Aunt Jane Austen: A Memoir" [1867], in J. E. Austen-Leigh, *A Memoir of Jane Austen and Other Family Recollections*, ed. Kathryn Sutherland (Oxford: Oxford University Press, 2002), 170.

7. Anna Lefroy, "Recollections of Aunt Jane" [1864], in Austen-Leigh, *A Memoir of Jane Austen*, 160.

8. Caroline Austen, in Austen-Leigh, *A Memoir of Jane Austen*, 169.

9. Ibid., 173.

10. Cicero, *On the Ideal Orator* (*De Oratore* 1.32), trans. James M. May and Jakob Wisse (New York: Oxford University Press, 2001), 65.

speak not only from duty, but also from enjoyment.[11] And yet count-less generations living prior to the twentieth century did just that. Jane Austen herself, the seventh of eight children in her family, was—like any younger sibling—first a listener. Beyond the banter of her brothers, there was much to attend to. In those days, letters were often read out loud, and, if Mr. Bennet's handling of Mr. Collins's corre-spondence is in any way indicative, could even be a source of genuine mirth. Books, too, were read in company: "My father," Austen wrote in her early twenties, "reads Cowper to us in the evening."[12] Indeed, her father's talent may have been the original for Henry Crawford's acumen as a reader of Shakespeare in the parlor at Mansfield Park, a talent capable of moving Fanny Price, in spite of her fear and suspi-cion of him.[13] Unlike Crawford's acting, which was also very skillful, his reading could be enjoyed as an honest pleasure: "To *good* reading," the narrator tells us, "she had long been used . . . but in Mr. Craw-ford's reading there was a variety of excellence beyond what she had ever met with."[14] Indeed, one of the most surprising aspects of Jane Austen's novels is how much attention is paid to listening and how much we are asked to notice what conversation reveals of her charac-ters. The grammatical faux-pas of Lucy Steele, the gaucherie of Mrs. Elton, the shrill blubbering of Mrs. Bennet, and the "large, fat sigh-ings" of Mrs. Musgrove: many are the utterances the hearing of which bring us pain. The duty of listening, and of listening charitably even when it costs an effort, is one of the central themes of *Emma*, the crux of which comes on Box Hill, when the young heroine can at last no longer restrain herself and mocks Miss Bates for her habit of nattering on. When Mr. Knightley taxes her with having acted in the "pride of the moment" and having been "insolent in her wit," Emma cannot fail

---

11. See Michael D. Aeschliman, "The Cold, Gray Glow: Television Comes to the Tuscan Hills," *Harpers* (December 1985), 71–72.

12. Jane Austen, *Selected Letters*, ed. R. W. Chapman (Oxford: Oxford University Press, 1985), 27.

13. See David Cecil, *A Portrait of Jane Austen* (New York: Farrar, Strauss, Giroux, 1979), 35, 46

14. Austen, *Mansfield Park*, ed. James Kinsley (Oxford: Oxford University Press, 2003), 264.

to acknowledge her fault.[15] However much the ridiculous was blended in with the good in Miss Bates, her condition in life made patient listening to her a strict duty. What was Miss Bates's fault, after all, than that of overestimating her audience's interest in matters she took to be worth mentioning? Every parent with a young child knows that there is hardly a more common failing. And is it not the case that, as one astute critic has pointed out, we as readers of Miss Bates's prattle are tempted by and are likely to succumb to the same annoyance that trumped Emma's forbearance?[16]

Austen's novels not only provide examples of the duty of listening to trifles, they also offer examples of silent reflection upon things said and heard. Her most striking illustration of the virtue of attentiveness is Anne Elliot, the heroine of *Persuasion*, who scarcely speaks to Captain Wentworth before the story's surprising ending, and who, prized as a confidante, must listen in pain to what she is told by her younger sister, her brother-in-law, Captain Hargrove, and her old school friend Mrs. Smith, before the great reversal when she is cast in the role of speaker and Captain Wentworth learns by listening. Yet Anne Elliot's attentiveness is not passivity. She, almost alone among Austen's heroines, strengthens herself with a moment of recollection that we recognize as prayer. And when the situation dictates action, she acts decisively, as when she is the only one capable of reacting properly to Louisa Musgrove's fall and, later, when she risks the charge of forwardness by addressing Captain Wentworth directly when she had not yet been spoken to by him. Her speech, when it comes, is measured and mature; her conversation with Captain Benwick, for instance, is a model of self-command, as she listens in order to understand and speaks in order to bring consolation. One is tempted to see in Anne Elliot's conversation the imitation of Austen's friend and mentor, Mrs. Anne Lefroy, whom she memorialized in these verses:

---

15. Austen, *Emma*, ed. James Kinsley (Oxford: Oxford University Press, 2003), 293–96.
16. See Peter W. Graham, *Jane Austen and Charles Darwin: Naturalists and Novelists* (Burlington, VT: Ashgate, 2008), 37.

> She speaks! 'Tis eloquence, that grace of tongue,
> So rare, so lovely, never misapplied
> By her, to palliate vice, or deck a wrong:
> She speaks and argues but on virtue's side.
> Hers is the energy of soul sincere;
> Her Christian spirit, ignorant to feign,
> Seeks but to comfort, heal, enlighten, cheer,
> Confer a pleasure or prevent a pain.[17]

These lovely lines express Jane Austen's conviction about the importance of careful and considerate speech. As a careful scholar of her work observed: "The ultimate propriety on which all other proprieties depended was [to her] a true propriety of language."[18] Exaggeration, display, the intemperate use of the first-person, and deceit: these are the verbal faults of Willoughby, Mary Crawford, and Mrs. Elton.[19] Jane Austen's most amiable characters—among whom Anne Elliot, Mrs. Gardiner, and Fanny Price stand out—speak the truth plainly and charitably and are able to do so because of an inner quiet of self-command. In this they are like their maker, who, as has often been observed, stood before human nature as a most attentive and respectful observer, a transparent witness to the things she saw and heard because her own judgment was unclouded. In both Jane Austen's craft and in her characters we are given models of attentiveness that can help us to take the necessary first steps in rebuilding a culture of the word.

Tuning the Word

If attentiveness is the characteristic virtue of the apprentice, then a more active excellence will be expected of the fully trained craftsman,

---

17. Jane Austen, "To the Memory of Mrs. Lefroy," [1808] in Austen-Leigh, *A Memoir of Jane Austen*, 49–50.

18. Tony Tanner, *Jane Austen* (Cambridge, MA: Harvard University Press, 1986), 20.

19. See Mary Lascelles, *Jane Austen and Her Art*, corrected edition (1939; Oxford: Oxford University Press, 1970), 50, 111–12.

the journeyman. In a culture of the word, such a craftsman will not only listen to words, he will be able to fashion a thing made of them, a poem. "Poetical" was the word that Newman used to describe the "old monastic life" of the Benedictines—a life of contemplation, liturgical prayer, and rustic labor that he thought could even be qualified as "Virgilian."[20] Benedict XVI sounds a similar note. "Because in the biblical word God comes towards us and we towards him," the Holy Father explains, "we must learn to penetrate the secret of language, to understand it in its construction and in the manner of its expression."[21] These are the skills of the poet, a craftsman whose task it is to tune the word, to make it both lovely to hear and luminously intelligible. To T. S. Eliot, the poet's function is a kind of mediation between experience and language. In great poetry, he suggested, "there is always the communication of some new experience, or some fresh understanding of the familiar, or the experience of something we have experienced but have no words for, which enlarges our consciousness or refines our sensibility." These benefits accrue to great poetry because it is the product of a language that has been well-tuned. Accordingly, to Eliot, the proper duty of the poet was "first to preserve, and second to extend and improve" his language.[22] The poet's labors, then, can promote a culture of the word, if they make available to his listeners and readers the "secrets" of their native tongue. As an illustration, we might take the work of Shakespeare, which, as Jane Austen's Henry Crawford explained, "is part of an English-man's constitution. His thoughts and beauties are so spread abroad that one touches them everywhere, one is intimate with him by instinct."[23] To be intimate with Shakespeare's words is, arguably, to have gained an ability to use the English language that is more adequate to the tasks that confront us as creatures who live by our wits.

---

20. Newman, "Mission of St. Benedict," 388, 409.

21. Benedict XVI, Address at the Collège des Bernadins.

22. T. S. Eliot, "The Social Function of Poetry," in *On Poetry and Poets* (New York: Farrar, Straus and Cudahy, 1957), 7, 9.

23. Austen, *Mansfield Park*, ed. Kinsley, 264–65.

It is not Shakespeare, however, but a poet of the French Renaissance, Jean de la Ceppède, that I would propose as an example of the special role that poetry can play in building up a culture of the word. His comparative anonymity may even be a help, as it forces us to consider the poet in his work, where his craftsmanship, and little else, is to be seen. Of his life, it suffices to say that he was a high-ranking judge in the regional court at Aix-en-Provence, where he belonged to an illustrious circle of humanists. It was in 1594, at the end of the French Wars of Religion, that La Ceppède published his first work, an *Imitation of the Penitential Psalms of David*. In a dedicatory epistle that was an extended meditation upon the theme of "shipwreck," he declared his desire to "dispose his soul and, with it, poor France" to look to the Cross for safety and to take "the good David" as guide for "this perilous navigation."[24] To paraphrase or imitate the Psalms was a common undertaking in those days. La Ceppède's efforts may be likened to those of some of the best-known poets of the period, including his friend Malherbe (Psalm 146), the Castilian friar Luis de Léon (Psalm 130), and George Herbert (Psalm 23).[25] The recitation of the seven penitential psalms (Psalms 6, 33, 38, 51, 102, 130, and 143) was then a popular Lenten practice, and La Ceppède's imitations, each accompanied with a lengthy prayer, succeed in expressing the sentiments of a contrite and humble heart. The work also included a number of other poems, including twelve sonnets that he offered in the hope that "they would give some consolation to Christian souls amidst the numerous evils that they suffer" and as an advanced offering from a more ambitious task upon which he was already laboring, the *Theorems upon the Sacred Mystery of Our Redemption*.[26]

This was La Ceppède's life's work, a great cycle of 515 sonnets upon the theme of the Passion, Death, and Resurrection of Christ; it

---

24 Jean de la Ceppède, *Imitation des Psaumes de la Penitence de David* (Lyon: Jean Tholosan, 1594), 1–3.

25 On which theme, see Louis Martz, *The Poetry of Meditation* (New Haven: Yale University Press, 1954), 273–82.

26 La Ceppède, *Imitation*, 39.

was published in two parts, the first in 1613 and the second in 1622. The *Theorems* is not only poetry, it is a splendid work of erudition, for each sonnet is provided with a commentary linking it to Scriptural and Patristic sources and, especially, to the *Summa Theologiae* of St. Thomas Aquinas. The work bears the mark of the Renaissance: the sonnet, that choice mode of expressing romantic love, is here purged and elevated and put in the service of the epic tale of God's love for man. As La Ceppède put it in his introduction—which can be read in Keith Bosley's admirable translation of seventy of the sonnets— the harlot Lady Poetry had been unstitched of "her worldly habits" and shorn of her "idolatrous, lying and lascivious hair" by the "two-edged razor of profound meditation on the Passion and death of our Saviour."[27] Deeply thoughtful the work certainly is. The title's operative word, theorem, calls to mind the propositions of Euclid's *Elements of Geometry*, and the parallel is not far-fetched. Euclid isolated the properties of geometrical figures and delighted in tying down to their proper principles not only noble truths such as the one disclosed in the Pythagorean Theorem, but also truths more modest yet still fruitful for the science. In similar fashion, La Ceppède took a verse or two, or at times a single word, an action, or an aspect of a person's character from the Gospels—some of them obviously significant, others less so—and subjected his choice to a brief but penetrating consideration. The choice of the sonnet was a happy one: the discipline of keeping to fourteen lines of twelve syllables made the meditations sharply focused.[28] The sonnet form did not, however, force the poems into dull uniformity. He employed differing rhyme schemes, relieved the monotony of end-stopped lines with the periodic use of enjambment, and repeatedly changed his rhythm and tone. The sonnets also change in their mode of address: most are impersonal meditations, but many are prayers to Christ, and still others are addressed directly

---

27. La Ceppède's introduction "To France," in *From the Theorems of Master Jean de La Ceppède: LXX Sonnets*, a bilingual edition translated with an introduction by Keith Bosley (Mid Northumberland Arts Group, Ashington, UK, 1983), 17.

28. See Terence C. Cave, *Devotional Poetry in France, c. 1570–1613* (Cambridge: Cambridge University Press, 1969), 237, 242.

to the listener as to a faithful Christian soul, or to one or more of the apostles. Some of the sonnets are particularly melodious, such as the one exploring Christ's posture while at prayer in the Garden of Gethsemane that begins: "*L'humblesse est le rayon qui perce le nuage* / Humility is the ray that pierces the cloud." (The French is antique, but no less musical for that.) Others employ repetition to drive the theme home, such as the white sonnet, in which ten lines begin with *blanc* or *blanche*, and other sonnets devoted to the role of the angels or the significance of the number three. The sonnets, on the whole, are characterized by directness and a desire for clarity, signs of which are ready to hand in the often lengthy footnotes providing theological justifications for his choice of words.

In order better to appreciate both his art and the depth of his religious feeling, let us consider in full the striking sonnet that reflects upon just two words of Scripture, Pilate's line "Ecce homo."

Behold the Man, O my eyes, what a deplorable sight!
Shame, sleeplessness, lack of food,
Sorrows, and so much blood lost
Have left him deformed and undesirable.
    That hair (the ornament of his venerable head)
Bloodied, stood on end by this coronation,
Tangled in these reeds, serves unworthily
To his injured head as an execrable fence.
    Those eyes (once so lovely) beaten, retreated,
Sunken in, are, alas, two suns in eclipse.
The coral of his mouth is now pale yellow.
    The roses and lilies of his skin are faded.
The rest of his body is the color of opal,
So bruised are his members from head to feet.[29]

In the French, the sonnet is not harmonious. La Ceppède labored against the native fluidity of the language by multiplying hard con-

---

29. Jean de la Ceppède, *Les Théorèmes sur le Sacré Mystère de notre Rédemption: Reproduction de l'édition de Toulouse de 1613-1622* (Geneva: Droz, 1966), 304–5.

sonants and acute accents and interrupting the flow of the poem with many inserted stops. The tone and mood of the sonnet match the sentiment expressed, which is of one who is, like Christ, appalled. If one were to read this sonnet in isolation from those that express different emotions, such as the heroic *Love brought him from Olympus here below* or the lovely and compassionate *He has climbed up, my love, upon the gibbet ordained*—one might conclude that La Ceppède's vision was merely bleak and, certainly, watery and thin. Yet when we see that the last line of the first quatrain is a deliberate echo of Isaiah 53:2, "he had . . . no beauty that we should desire him," then we are offered a glimpse of his ability to "enlarge our consciousness"—in Eliot's phrase—by a faithful and efficacious exploration of the Word. It is a sonnet, I think, that perfectly expresses what the onlooker ought to have felt at that moment and captures the full import of Pilate's command to "behold the man." To meditate upon the various scenes of the Passion in the company of Jean de La Ceppède's *Theorems upon the Sacred Mystery of Our Redemption* is, then, to be made attuned to the very words of Holy Scripture. The work is a splendid instance of the poet's craft serving the life of contemplation—the life of conversation with God—and building up a culture of the word.

Performing the Word

A truly living culture of the word requires not only that we attend to the word and enter into thoughtful conversation with it, but also that the word "dwell in [us] richly," in St. Paul's lovely phrase. (Col. 3:16) Echoing the Apostle, Benedict XVI explains that in a culture of the word "speech is not enough," but that "music is required," music fitting to be sung "in the presence of the angels." (Psalm 138:1) "The culture of singing" that was and is the Benedictine culture of the word, "is also the culture of being," the Holy Father emeritus tells us, because "the monks have to pray and sing in a manner commensurate with the grandeur of the word handed down to them, with its claim on true beauty." This phrase "culture of being" opens the dimension of moral action. The word of God is not given us as a recondite object for scholars alone to ponder, but as the word of life, to be acted upon, even acted out, by ordinary men and women. The Word is, as Benedict's XVI put it in *Spe Salvi*, "not only informative, but performative."

It is most fitting to end a reflection upon the ways in which the life of study, reading, and writing can help to prepare the way for a renewed culture of the word by considering an instance of the dramatic art. The Church's culture of the word is found preeminently in the sacred liturgy, an act at once profoundly imitative and supremely efficacious. Those who have been present for the solemn and due celebration of the Easter Vigil Mass can readily conjure up images of the manifold artistry that accompanies and surrounds the liturgical performance of the word. So rich a feast for the imagination is the liturgy, with its annual commemoration of the saving deeds of Christ, that the faithful through the ages have repeatedly found in it the inspiration for works of dramatic imitation both great and small. To consider only the greatest genius in this vein, let us recall the holy imitation of St. Francis of Assisi, who naïvely acted upon Christ's message to him by rebuilding the church of San Damiano with trowel in hand, brought the custom of imitating Christ's Way of the Cross from the Holy Land back to Europe, and, in the little hamlet of Grecchio, re-enacted that first Christmas with ox and ass and straw and song and thus gave birth to our colorful tradition of Christmas pageants and caroling. In St. Francis, imitation—acting—and reality were folded together in ways marvelous, even strange, but his imitation was blessed by God, who, at the end of his life, gave him no mere costume to wear, but imprinted upon his body the very wounds of Christ. In the centuries after St. Francis, many Christian writers followed him in spirit by producing works that enabled the dramatic performance of the word. In England, there were the mystery and miracle plays written for the feast of Corpus Christi, which provided a form of narrative catechesis that was both compelling and lastingly effective. In Spain, the tradition of sacred drama produced works still performed and admired today, such as the *autos sacramentales* of Pedro Calderon de la Barca, author of that most winning of morality plays, *Life Is a Dream* (1635). It was in

France, however, that the encounter between the Word of God and a great playwright produced what is arguably the masterpiece of the genre, Jean Racine's *Athalie*.

Racine is surely one of the greatest examples of one who embraced the life of writing as a craft.[30] Orphaned at a tender age, he was raised by an extraordinary group of priests and scholars, the solitaries who lived just outside the walls of the monastery of Port-Royal des Champs, generally referred to as the Jansenists. They gave him an education that was overwhelmingly linguistic and literary. It was not unusual in those days for an educated man to read, speak, and compose in Latin as well as or even better than in French. Racine could do this, and more. By the age of eighteen, he not only also read Spanish and Italian, but, crucially, he had full command of ancient Greek. And these languages he knew not as dead, but as living. He annotated his Greek text of Plutarch's *Lives* with maxims to live by while committing Virgil's *Aeneid* to memory and writing his own lyric poems in both Latin and French. Racine brought to this rich humanistic course of study both astonishing linguistic ability and a mind that took deep impressions of what it encountered. An anecdote from much later in his life serves to illustrate the way in which his education made the Classics a living part of him. "He was in Auteuil, at the house of Boileau," as his son tells the story,

> when they came to be speaking of Sophocles, of whom he was so great an admirer that he had never dared to take one of his stories for his own tragedies. Full of [admiration], he took up a Greek Sophocles, and read the tragedy of Oedipus, translating it on the spot. He was so moved . . . that all of the auditors felt the sentiments of fervor and pity of which the play is full. "I have seen," [said one who was there] "our best plays performed by our best actors: nothing ever approached the trouble into which this

---

30 Racine's commitment to and practice of what his friend Boileau called "le métier du poëte" is one of the central themes of Georges Forestier, *Jean Racine* (Paris: Gallimard, 2006).

recitation cast my spirit; and . . . I can still see Racine, book in hand, and all of us around him, moved by sorrow."[31]

It was an astounding display of erudition and theatrical ability. To move his audiences with stirring words: this was the young Racine's goal and his gift. Between 1664 and 1677, he achieved both wealth and lasting fame by doing so repeatedly with masterpieces such as *Andromaque* and *Phèdre*, both modeled after plays by Euripides.

The years of his triumphs on the Paris stage are the lost years for his biographer: just a single handful of letters remains from his correspondence during that period. It does seem incontestable that during these years his observance of the Catholic faith was irregular, certainly compared to the last twenty years of his life, during which he attended Mass daily and lived a model and devoted family life. After 1677, Racine was one of the official historiographers at the court of Louis XIV, his great patron. It was to please the king's consort, Madame de Maintenon, that Racine wrote two biblical dramas, a modest three-act play based upon the central events of the Book of Esther in 1689, and two years later, a full-length play devoted to the tragic end of Jezebel's wicked daughter Athaliah.

This minor episode from the history of the kings of Juda was particularly suited for reenactment on the stage, for it is a story full of drama. Its tragic aspect is in the death of the idolatrous Queen Athaliah, who reaps the bitter harvest of her wickedness. Upon learning of the death of her son Ahaziah, she had fallen into a rage and attempted to kill all of her grandsons, the last of the line of David. She failed, however, and six years later, the lone heir to the throne and hope for the messianic promise, Joash, was living in the Temple under the care of his aunt, the Princess Josabet. Racine's play is a dramatization of, as he put it, "Joash recognized and placed upon the throne."[32] This action,

---

31. Louis Racine, *Vie de Racine* (Paris: Les Belles Lettres, 1999), 115–16.

32. Racine's preface to *Athalie*, in Jean Racine, *Oeuvres complètes, I: Théatre, Poésies*, ed. Raymond Picard (Paris: Gallimard, 1950), 872. All subsequent references to *Athalie* will be to this edition and will be made parenthetically in the text by reference to act, scene, and line number.

while deadly to Athaliah, was the triumph of the play's great hero, the high priest Joad. The biblical narratives describing the episode (2 Kings 11 and 2 Chronicles 22–23) are spare. Racine, however, did not scruple to imagine a likely confrontation between the two great moral characters of the prophetic and courageous high priest and the imperious and ruthless Queen. He added depth to Athaliah's character by portraying her as less wicked than her counselor, the apostate Levite turned priest of Baal, Mathan, who manipulated her by playing upon her "insatiable thirst for gold." Racine also invented the episode of a dream in which Athaliah saw the bloodied members of her mother Jezebel torn apart by dogs and then a youth robed in priestly garments, who thrust a dagger into her heart. The dream overmastered her, as Racine had her express in powerful lines reminiscent of some of his earlier poetry:

> A dream (should I be made anxious by a dream?)
> Keeps my heart bound with gnawing pain.
> I flee it everywhere, everywhere it pursues me.

When Athaliah first sees the young Joash in the Temple, not knowing his identity, she nevertheless recognizes him as the youth from her dream, and her equilibrium is destroyed. From this weakness stems her inability to respond to Joad's plot with her customary effectiveness. The high priest lures her into the Temple later that day for the unveiling of Joash as crowned and anointed king. Athaliah, surrounded by armed Levites, is helpless; she is dragged from the Temple precinct and executed, and the priest of Baal is put to the sword.

Racine's drama turns upon the central action of the unveiling of Joash, but the young king himself is not the one responsible for that action. It is his uncle, the high priest, who stands as the mirror image of the wicked Queen. While Athaliah's sins have made her irresolute, Joad's faithfulness has given him heroic courage. Athaliah chiefly suffers; it is Joad who acts, preparing and springing the trap that topples the persecuting tyrant. What is most relevant to our present concern, however, is less the structure of the plot or even the character of Joad but the means by which he accomplishes his task, which is by speech. As is often the case in classical tragedy, fell deeds are kept off-stage and reported second-hand. On the stage are characters who confront the challenges that face them not so much by swordplay, fisticuffs, or fancy shooting—techniques to be exploited to our great delight by the cinema—but by speeches in which their actions are prepared, incited, described, and—crucially—specified in their goodness or wickedness by the disclosure of their motives. Racine is, perhaps, most famous for the struggles of his tragic protagonists against the passions that enslave them; yet he was also, like his contemporary Corneille, a playwright who thrilled audiences by the heroic orations of his virtuous characters. Joad's charge to the Levites deserves to be placed alongside Henry V's speech on St. Crispin's Day. It has been unusually well translated by John Cairncross:

> Here then is your new king, your only hope;
> I have preserved him for you, till this day.
> Servants of God, the last act is for you.
> Soon will the murderous child of Jezebel,
> Learning that Joash here is still alive,
> Return to plunge him back into the tomb.
> Already, without knowing him, she seeks
> To slaughter him. You must forestall her rage.
> Finish the shameful bondage of the Jews,
> Avenge your princes' death, restore your law,
> And force both tribes to recognize their king.
> The enterprise is great and perilous.
> It's to attack an overweening queen,
> Beneath whose banner march unnumbered hordes
> Of reckless foreigners and turncoat Jews.
> In God whose interest guides me is my strength.
> Remember, in this child all Israel dwells!
> Already an avenging God begins
> To cloud her mind. I have, outwitting her,
> Assembled you. She thinks you here unarmed.
> Let us proclaim and crown young Joash now.

Then, valiant soldiers of our newfound prince,
March, calling on the Lord of Battles' name,
And, stirring faith anew in slumbering hearts,
Even in her palace seek our enemy.
And what faint hearts plunged in a craven sleep,
Seeing us in this holy band come on,
Will not at once fall into step and fight?
A king that in His temple God has reared,
Aaron's successor, followed by his priests,
Leading the sons of Levi on to war
Who hold in their own hands the arms revered
That David consecrated to the Lord.
God will spread terror on his enemies.
Wade staunchly in the blood of infidels.
Cut down the Tyrians; smite the Israelites.

. . .

But even now you burn to follow me.
Swear, above all, upon this sacred book
To the king heaven restores to you this day,
For him to live, to battle, and to die.[33]

It was, perhaps, with a passage just such as this in mind that Louis de Bonald, a close student of Racine's plays, once said that "dramatic poetry heightens and ornaments the moral world by giving virtue the character of heroism."[34] What Racine was able to accomplish in this speech, and in *Athalie* as a whole, was to make available to his readers and, especially, to spectators at a performance of the tragedy, the high moral drama that is in the Scripture itself. His play invites us not only to contemplate, but to imitate and to perform the lofty ideals and sentiments of the Word of God.

33.. Jean Racine, *Iphigenia, Phaedra, Athaliah*, trans. John Cairncross (London: Penguin, 1963), 297–98. I have taken the liberty of restoring the order of Racine's words in the final line.

34. Louis de Bonald, "Sur l'independence des gens de lettres," in *Oeuvres de Monsieur de Bonald* (Bruxelles: Société Nationale pour la propagation des Bons Livres, 1845), VII:49–50.

A Concluding Reflection

In his address at the *Collège des Bernadins,* Benedict XVI proposed the monastic culture of the word as a fruitful model for spiritual renewal in our time. In the monks' studious life, the interpretation of, meditation upon, and living out of the Scriptures was prepared and shaped by the traditional arts of the trivium: logic and, especially, grammar and rhetoric. In pursuit of those arts, the monks read and memorized and imitated the poems of Virgil and the letters of Cicero, among many other texts, using those pagan works as a kind of cultural preparation for the Gospel. These studies made them more attentive to speech, more aware of the nuances of language, and better able to appreciate the dramatic significance of texts, and these skills or virtues in turn helped them to apprehend, to internalize, and to celebrate the saving message of God's word. It is, therefore, a vindication of literary studies to affirm, with the Holy Father, that it was through the monks' "search for God that the secular sciences [took] on their importance." Such a claim about the fruitfulness of the due ordering of the different fields of study follows directly in the footsteps of Aquinas, who expressed the more general principle in this way: "Every science and art is ordered to one [end], namely to the perfection of man, which is his beatitude."[35] Having seen the congruence of their works to the habits and practices of the monastic culture of the word, we may say in conclusion, that common to the artistry of Jane Austen, Jean de la Ceppède, and Jean Racine is a certain openness or even fittingness to ends beyond the ones they had immediately in view. When artisans of the word ply their craft as these three did, with minds open and attentive to what nature—the divine art—discloses about the good, with the tools of their craft reverently cleaned and honed, and with the pur-

---

35. St. Thomas Aquinas, *Commentary on Aristotle's* Metaphysics, Prooemium: "Omnes autem scientiae et artes ordinantur in unum, scilicet ad hominis perfectionem, quae est eius beatitudo."

pose of producing works that would elevate the minds of those who read them, they may be sure that their efforts will not be drowned out amidst the clamor of the world, but will be heard as echoes of that first word from which all true words take their origin.

7

The Historian's Tools

WHEN POPE GREGORY IX wrote to the masters and scholars of the university at Paris in 1231, he likened the young institution to a jeweler's shop, calling it an *officina sapientiae*, a workshop of wisdom.[1] His phrase brings to mind an image of the liberal arts as so many fine tools—honed, oiled, neatly arranged, and ready at hand—and of craftsmen deftly using them while considering man's nature and his end, the order of the universe, and the mysteries of God and of the divine economy. This is a most satisfying image of an institution rightly called "the glory of the middle ages."[2] Even if we were to decide that St. Thomas Aquinas did not so much typify the medieval university as he did exemplify the wisdom toward which its practices were meant to be ordered, even if, that is, we were to prescind from a definitive judgment in favor of the medieval university as the ideal institution of higher learning, it would nevertheless present for us one of the most important markers in our search to understand the task of education. As we look back upon it, one of the aspects of the medieval university that strikes us is that it made no place in its ranks for the kind of craftsman we have come to call the historian. To one who practices the

---

1. Gregory IX, *Parens scientiarum*, in Heinrich Denifle, O.P., *Chartularium Universitatis Parisiensis*, I (Paris, 1899; Bruxelles: Culture et Civilisation, 1964), 137.

2. John Henry Newman, *The Idea of a University*, ed. Martin J. Svaglic (Notre Dame, IN: University of Notre Dame Press, 1982), 13.

craft, this fact should be an occasion of wonder. And so it is with fear and hope intertwined that the historian inquires of the tradition what role he and his tools might fulfill in the workshop of wisdom.

In approaching the question, it would be difficult to find a better guide than the Blessed John Henry Newman. In the first place, Newman has been recommended to us by St. John Paul II as a "sure and eloquent guide in our perplexity" and as one who achieved a "remarkable synthesis of faith and reason."[3] We can take additional confidence from Newman's own description of what has been called the "intellectual custom" of the Church.[4] "Catholic inquiry," he wrote, in the final chapter of his *Apologia*, "has taken certain definite shapes, and has thrown itself into the form of a science, with a method and a phraseology of its own, under the intellectual handling of great minds, such as St. Athanasius, St. Augustine, and St. Thomas; and I feel no temptation at all to break in pieces the great legacy of thought thus committed to us for these latter days."[5] In light of this beautiful statement of his fidelity to the mind of the Church, may we not suppose that Newman himself would wish to stand for us not so much as an authority in his own right, but as a witness to the Catholic intellectual tradition? His great value lies in his faithful and creative transmission of what he himself received, and so he is able not only to shed light on historical study, but also to exemplify the virtues that a Catholic historian ought to cultivate.

As we attempt to learn from his example, let us first consider the role that historical study played in his conversion, then attend to his reflection upon the place of historical study within a liberal education, and, finally, sketch an answer to the question of the historian's role in the workshop of wisdom today.

---

3. John Paul II, "Letter on the Occasion of the 2nd Centenary of the Birth of Cardinal John Henry Newman" (January 22, 2001), (www.vatican.va).

4. See Ronald McArthur, "Saint Thomas and the Formation of the Catholic Mind," in *The Ever-Illuminating Wisdom of St. Thomas Aquinas* (San Francisco: Ignatius Press, 1999), 123–43.

5. John Henry Newman, *Apologia Pro Vita Sua*, ed. Ian Ker (London: Penguin, 1994), 224–25.

Deep in History

As even a casual glance at his *Essay on the Development of Christian Doctrine* reveals, Newman's historical erudition was immense. By the time of his conversion in 1845, he had been studying the Church Fathers for the better part of two decades; indeed, he tells the story of his conversion partially in terms of the progress of his historical studies and of the changes they wrought in his mind. The contrast between Newman's *Apologia Pro Vita Sua* and Augustine's *Confessions* helps to underscore the importance of history to Newman's conversion. Augustine had long lived an unchristian life, held the simplicity of the Christian scriptures to be a mark against them, and labored under metaphysical errors inculcated by the Manichean sect. Newman faced entirely different obstacles to right belief. He had been "brought up from a child to take great delight in reading the Bible," and at the age of fifteen had experienced a conversion to an evangelical form of Christianity that sealed him in moral earnestness and gave to him the great gift of being able in prayer to "rest in the thought of two and two only absolute and luminously self-evident beings, myself and my Creator."[6] And so, we might say that Augustine discovered Christ and his Church together, whereas Newman, born and baptized an Anglican, knew Christ from birth, but had to travel a long and often painful road to find him in his fullness in the Roman Catholic Church, the Church of all the ages, the Church of history.

When Newman first went up to Oxford in 1817, he was an awkward youth of sixteen. Serious and studious, he disapproved of his fellow students' carousing. "If any one should ask me what qualifications were necessary for Trinity College," he wrote to his father, "I should say there was only one, —Drink, drink, drink."[7] After three abstemious years of poring over Euclid and Sophocles, Aristotle and Cicero, he took his bachelor's degree, and, then, after two more years of study and teaching, was elected a Fellow of Oriel College in 1822. There

---

6. Ibid., 25.

7. Newman's letter to his father, quoted in Ian T. Ker, *John Henry Newman: A Biography* (Oxford: Clarendon Press, 1988), 7.

he came under the influence of two older dons, Edward Hawkins and Richard Whately. Newman credited these two mentors—the latter of them famously devoted to Aristotle's logical works—with having taught him "to weigh my words" and "to think and to use my reason." They also introduced him to the importance of tradition in Christianity by convincing him that the faith of the Church, expressed in her creeds, was prior to the Bible, or, in Newman's words, "that the sacred text was never intended to teach doctrine, but only to prove it."[8] Whately also conveyed to Newman a conviction that the church was by its nature independent from the state, a particularly momentous truth to a member of the church established by the laws of King Henry VIII and his daughter Queen Elizabeth.

It was the threat posed to the Church of England by the Reform Bill of 1832 and associated legislation that occasioned the protest against political liberalism that became the Oxford Movement. Newman had by then long been thrown into the company of John Keble, a country priest from a conservative clerical family who was also a Fellow of Oriel, and the author of The Christian Year, a popular volume of devotional poetry. Whereas the influence of Hawkins and Whately had threatened to make Newman—as he put it—"prefer intellectual excellence to moral," in Keble he found "a religious teaching" that was "deep, pure, and beautiful," and also a fervent belief in "the Sacramental system" and in the communion of saints.[9] When Keble sounded the alarm in 1833 with his sermon "National Apostasy," the Oxford Movement was born. Its principle was simple: Since non-Anglicans could now vote for and sit in Parliament, the Church of England had to find a more stable foundation for itself than it enjoyed in English law, and that foundation would be its antiquity, its claim to apostolic succession.

From its inception, however, the Oxford Movement was always as much a spiritual revival as it was a movement of ecclesiastical politics. Thanks to Keble's influence, Newman's youthful evangelical zeal had now been combined with a love for tradition. As a boy, he had stum-

---

8. *Apologia Pro Vita Sua*, 29–31.

9. Ibid., 36–37.

bled across a history of the early church and had ever since nourished an almost romantic attachment to the age of the Fathers. Now as a mature scholar and priest, he sought in the early church a source of inspiration for a renewed Anglicanism: "We were upholding that primitive Christianity which was delivered for all time by the early teachers of the Church, and which was registered and attested in the Anglican formularies and by the Anglican divines." The signal achievement of the first half of the Oxford Movement was an enthusiastic reclaiming of the spiritual heritage of the early church. Not only were the teachings of the Fathers to be published "in fullest measure," but, as Newman put it, "the middle age belonged to the Anglican Church" too, and "much more did the middle age of England." So from Newman's pen came forth a study of the Arians of the Fourth Century and a series of vignettes on saints, such as Anthony of the Desert and Augustine, later published under the title The Church of the Fathers, intended to bring "the religious sentiments, views, and customs of the first ages into the modern Church of England."[10]

Meanwhile, Newman's colleague E. B. Pusey began an ambitious project to produce a "great flood of divinity" with a Library of the Fathers.[11] And, spurred on by all this study, the Oxford Movement led to liturgical changes—such as the revival of public morning prayer—and a deepening of personal piety in its members, including, for some, the regular use of the Roman Breviary.[12] It was a great experiment to see whether a Protestant church could accept the full measure of primitive Christianity, and for a time it seemed as though the experiment might succeed. All of this backwards looking, after all, was in keeping with the sensibility of a generation that had been raised on the novels of Sir Walter Scott, which, in Newman's words, had answered the need of the day for "something deeper and more attractive" and had "silently indoctrinat[ed]" their readers "with nobler ideas."[13]

---

10 Ibid., 57, 67, 78, 80 – 81.

11 Newman, quoted in Ker, *John Henry Newman*, 134.

12 For these and other instances, see ibid., 103, 145, 159–60, 166.

13. *Apologia Pro Vita Sua*, 99.

In the end, Newman's experiment failed. The bishops of the Church of England rejected his interpretation of its authoritative doctrinal document, the Thirty-Nine Articles of Religion. But, even before he suffered rebukes from authorities he revered, Newman's own faith in the Church of England had already been called into question by his historical studies. In the summer of 1839, he had plunged into the history of the Monophysite heresy of the fifth century. What he found there was, on the one hand, a heretical movement making a claim of antiquity in favor of its position and, on the other, a pope resolutely claiming to speak on behalf of the whole Church. In the struggles of the fifth century, Newman found "Christendom of the sixteenth and nineteenth centuries reflected. I saw my face in that mirror, and I was a Monophysite." Then, two years later, after the bishops had decided against him, he made a fresh study of the Arian heresy and "saw clearly, that in the history of Arianism, the pure Arians were the Protestants, the semi-Arians were the Anglicans, and that Rome now was what it was then."[14]

At the beginning of the Oxford Movement, Newman had taken "Antiquity, not the existing Church, as the oracle of truth." But his initial approach to antiquity had been faulty. He and his friends had aimed to give the Church of England "a second Reformation: —a better reformation," by returning "not to the sixteenth century, but to the seventeenth." They would purify Anglicanism not by a more stern application of the doctrines of Luther and Calvin—doctrines which they rejected—but by the careful study of the great English theologians of the seventeenth century, men such as the Anglican bishops William Laud, George Bull, and Lancelot Andrewes. It was that very faithfulness to his English Protestant heritage that had been the source of Newman's confusion: "I had read the Fathers with their eyes; I had sometimes trusted their quotations or their reasonings; and from reliance on them, I had used words or made statements, which by right I ought rigidly to have examined myself." Newman taxed himself with not having "read the Fathers cautiously enough." Now that he had lost

---

14. Ibid., 114, 134.

faith in the Church of England's claim to be the custodian of the doctrine of the early church, he had to turn to the Fathers again, this time to see whether their teaching had been faithfully preserved by the Church of Rome. At stake was his very belief, for he had come "to the conclusion that there was no medium, in true philosophy, between Atheism and Catholicity." The result of that unprejudiced rereading of the Fathers was his celebrated Essay on the Development of Christian Doctrine, his last work as a Protestant. This time the careful study of antiquity removed all of his doubts: "Before I got to the end, I resolved to be received."[15] John Henry Newman had discovered—as he put it—that "to be deep in history" was "to cease to be a Protestant."[16]

History and Liberal Education

Seeing the vital contribution to Newman's conversion made by his historical studies, one might well suppose that he would hold such studies to be the backbone of a liberal education. Plausible support for such a view can be found in his writings, as in this suggestive passage: "I saw that the principle of development not only accounted for certain facts, but was in itself a remarkable philosophical phenomenon, giving a character to the whole course of Christian thought."[17] And if one were to add to a regard for Newman a sense of the very real cultural poverty of modernity, one might very well conclude that a course of study in Christian culture is not only a necessary part of a Catholic liberal education, but its most important part.[18] Newman's own theoretical writings on education, however, do not confirm such

---

15. Ibid., 148, 157, 182, 186–87, 211.

16. John Henry Newman, *An Essay on the Development of Christian Doctrine*, 6th edition (London, 1878; reprinted Notre Dame, IN: University of Notre Dame Press, 1989), 8.

17. *Apologia Pro Vita Sua*, 182.

18. One might come to such a conclusion through a lopsided interpretation of Christopher Dawson's suggestion that the study of Christian culture serve as "a means of integration and unity" within a curriculum. See *The Crisis of Western Education* (New York: Sheed and Ward, 1961), 134.

a view. Even though he continued to study and write about the past after his conversion, he accorded the art of history a strictly subordinate role—not a ruling one—in the workshop of wisdom.

The abundance of Newman's creativity, the suppleness of his composition, and the harmoniousness of his language can hide from us the fact that the contours of his mind were essentially Aristotelian. In addition to containing his own affirmation that "in many subject matters, to think correctly, is to think like Aristotle," the fifth discourse of his *Idea of a University* testifies to his essentially Aristotelian conception of liberal education.[19] The kind of knowledge that a liberal education provides, he explained there, is not "Knowledge in a vague and ordinary sense," but the knowledge that is "especially called Philosophy." He developed the point by meditating on the distinction between what he called "mechanical knowledge," which is "exhausted upon what is particular and external" and ushers in the "useful or mechanical arts" on the one hand, and "philosophical" knowledge on the other, which "rises towards general ideas." What is generally called knowledge "in proportion as it tends more and more to be particular, ceases to be Knowledge" in this latter and true sense. By philosophical knowledge, Newman meant "something intellectual, something which grasps what is perceived through the senses; something which takes a view of things; which sees more than the senses convey; which reasons upon what it sees, and while it sees; which invests it with an idea. It expresses itself, not in a mere enunciation, but by an enthymeme: it is of the nature of science from the first, and in this consists its dignity." As a summary of the doctrine of the *Posterior Analytics*, this is perhaps a bit breezy. Yet, it is a faithful sketch of it for a popular audience. And consider, further, this echo of the doctrine of the sixth book of the *Nicomachean Ethics*: "Such knowledge is not a mere extrinsic or accidental advantage, which is ours today and another's tomorrow, which may be got up from a book, and easily forgotten again"; no, real philosophical knowledge "is a habit, a per-

---

19. *Idea of a University*, 83.

sonal possession, and an inward endowment."[20] And although, in the second discourse on "Theology a Branch of Knowledge," Newman did not explicitly refer to Aquinas or Aristotle, he nevertheless affirmed their conviction that the true terminus and resting place of human inquiry is the consideration of the eternal God as first cause and final end of all that exists when he defended what he called "the old Catholic notion" that "Faith was an intellectual act, its object truth, and its result knowledge."[21]

Holding, then, as he did, with Aristotle, that true knowledge consists in the understanding of principles and causes, and not merely in an extensive familiarity with phenomena or effects, Newman prescribed a form of education that would be conducive to philosophical knowledge, an education he called a "discipline in accuracy of mind."[22] In the bracing sixth discourse of *The Idea of a University* on "Knowledge viewed in Relation to Learning," as also in his separate treatments of "Elementary Studies" and "Discipline of Mind," Newman made an uncompromising defense of the old classical disciplines of the liberal arts that had shaped him during his undergraduate years and that he himself had tested as a tutor at Oriel in the 1820s. The first step in such an "intellectual training" was for the student's mind to be impressed with "the idea of science, method, order, principle, and system; of rule and exception, of richness and harmony."[23] Grammar, especially in a classical or foreign language, and mathematics were the best instruments to achieve these ends. Such a discipline can be nothing but painstaking: "Our rule is to recommend to youths to do a little well, instead of throwing themselves upon a large field of study."[24] And the reason for this slowness was the very character of authentic learning: "If we would improve the intellect, first of all, we must ascend; we cannot gain real knowledge on a level; we must generalize, we must

---

20. Ibid., 84-85.

21. Ibid., 21.

22. Newman, "Elementary Studies," in *Idea of a University*, 248.

23. *Idea of a University*, xliv.

24. "Elementary Studies," 263.

reduce to method, we must have a grasp of principles, and group and shape our acquisitions by means of them."[25]

Well did Newman appreciate the fact that this kind of arduous, careful study was no longer considered necessary. He was alarmed by the trend he saw toward "an unmeaning profusion of subjects," which he labeled "the error of distracting and enfeebling the mind." He railed against the common misconception of the day "to fancy that the gratification of a love of reading is real study."[26] And, in the context of a public lecture, he observed that "a man may hear a thousand lectures, and read a thousand volumes, and be at the end of the process very much where he was, as regards knowledge." Knowledge, he explained, to be real, "must not be passively received, but actually and actively entered into, embraced, mastered." Authentic, effective teaching, accordingly, is not mere lecturing, but is a "catechetical instruction, which consists in a sort of conversation between your lecturer and you."[27]

It might well be asked at this point what possible role a historian could play in the kind of education Newman was defending. And we have not yet heard the last of his admonitions. For the "memory can tyrannize," he warned, in a sort of prophecy of the contemporary culture of curiosity. But is not the historian's office one of remembering and of telling stories about the past? "I am not disparaging a well-stored mind," he continued, "nor am I banishing, far from it, the possessors of deep and multifarious learning from my ideal University; they adorn it in the eyes of men; I do but say that they constitute no type of the results at which it aims; that it is no great gain to the intellect to have enlarged the memory at the expense of faculties which are indisputably higher."[28] It seems a shame, and even something of an injustice, that a student should be trained up into becoming a historian, as he often is by the modern university. For while the achievements of specialists in this or that area of historical study are at times

---

25 *Idea of a University*, 105.

26. Ibid., 107, 255.

27. "Discipline of Mind," 368.

28. *Idea of a University*, 106–7.

very impressive, they all too often betray in one way or another the deficiencies of their own education. Newman foresaw that the shrinking of the mind would be the consequence of the modern university's trend toward specialization: "Although the art itself is advanced by this concentration of mind in its service, the individual who is confined to it goes back. The advantage of the community is nearly in an inverse ratio with his own."[29]

There is, however, some countervailing evidence in Newman's own writing and practice by which the defense of a certain kind of historian might be mounted. In his address on "Discipline of Mind," for instance, he asked his audience to "consider what a lesson in memory and discrimination it is to get up, as it is called, any one chapter of history."[30] And in the same discourse of the *Idea of a University* in which he warned against the tyranny of overloading the memory, he gave as one of the characteristics of the "perfection of the Intellect" that it was "almost prophetic from its knowledge of history." And, again, just a few pages earlier, he credited "the study of history" with a certain ability to enlarge and enlighten the mind, "because, as I conceive, it gives it a power of judging of past events."[31] The words "discrimination" and "judgment" suggest a habit of mind, an intellectual virtue, and not simply a well-stocked memory. In his tenure as rector of the Catholic University of Ireland, moreover, Newman invested a significant effort in historical writing. Just as his own study of the Church Fathers had removed the obstacles that stood in the way of his recognizing the teaching authority of the Catholic Church, so also did he prepare the Irish Catholic public to make a commitment to the high goal of liberal education by recounting for them its history, which he did in the twenty beautiful chapters of his *Rise and Progress of Universities*. Deep within that narrative is found a passage that in the present context presents a delightful irony, for it shows us Newman the histo-

---

29. Ibid., 127. This passage is part of a long, approving quotation from the writings of Edward Copleston.
30. "Discipline of Mind," 378.
31. *Idea of a University*, 99, 105.

rian discovering in the colleges of the medieval university—and then exercising his judgment by praising—the very system of education that seems to tell against the historian as we commonly meet him, that is, as a lecturer. Here is the conclusion to his account: "It is not easy for a young man to determine for himself whether he has mastered what he has been taught; a careful catechetical training, and a jealous scrutiny into his power of expressing himself and of turning his knowledge to account, will be necessary, if he is really to profit from the able Professors whom he is attending; and all this he will gain from the College Tutor."[32] If this passage is an example of the kind of principle of which historical study can somehow elicit acceptance, then perhaps even on pure Aristotelian grounds a role can be found for the historian and his tools in the workshop of wisdom.

The Office of the Historian

It will be well to begin with some distinctions. In the first place, let us set to the side the kind of teaching about the past that attempts to offer an interpretation of God's providential activity in this or that person, event, or trend. Such a reading of the signs of the times is of manifest importance for the Church, but it seems not to be the work of the historian as such, for the ability to do so is not gained through study or repeated practice; it seems rather to follow upon such causes as spiritual maturity, the gift of prophecy, and purity of heart. It is true that there are various scriptural principles that ought to shape any attempt to unravel the mysteries of providence: One thinks of the parable of the wheat and the tares (Mt 13:24–30), or Christ's promise to Peter that the "gates of hell shall not prevail" against the Church (Mt 16:18). But it seems that the application of these principles by those of us who are not Augustines ought to be highly tentative. And it certainly would be asking very much of historians to demand that they possess great spiritual gifts before practicing their craft.

---

32. *Rise and Progress of Universities*, in *Historical Sketches*, vol. III (London: Longmans, 1894), 190.

We should also set to the side the role of historical study in the various speculative disciplines and even within what might be called the speculative doctrine of the practical sciences. Aristotle tells us in the *Metaphysics*, among other places, that it is profitable to consider the views of those who have come before us in a given line of inquiry. Yet this kind of dialectical sifting of opinions is part of the way to the first principles and thus belongs to the science under consideration. Newman's own *Essay on Development* would seem to be an example of this kind of dialectical inquiry, for it begins with a generally acknowledged truth that the writings of the early Fathers are the essential intellectual records of the Christian faith, and then proceeds, at great length, to argue in favor of the conclusion that the Catholic Church teaches a doctrine in continuity with the Fathers. In proportion as an exposition employs arguments from the science in question—as Newman's certainly does—it belongs to the consideration of that science, and its author is called a theologian or philosopher rather than a historian. Our present concern, however, is not with the historical part of the various sciences, nor even with the mixed-breed called the "historian of," but with the jack-of-all-trades known simply as the historian.

There is broad, verbal agreement that historians are students of the past deeds of men and women. The accounts of this art, however, diverge from that point. This is not the place for a long, dialectical inquiry. In brief, however, we can say that the historian is not the possessor of a science in the strict sense, for "the contingency of historical events," as Glen Coughlin put it, "is incompatible with that certainty which accompanies what is knowable in the fullest sense."[33] The historian studies man and the acts of his free will, and if he generalizes at all, he makes claims that are irreducibly probabilistic and true with moral certitude at best. Nor should we think of history as the art of reconstructing the past for its own sake, for then we will indeed be tyrannized over by the faculty of memory and our historian will be little more than a walking encyclopedia. If Newman was

---

33. R. Glen Coughlin, "History and Liberal Education," *The Aquinas Review* 5 (1998): 22.

right to see in the good historian a faculty of right judgment, then history might best be understood as a subalternate part of ethics, and the writing of histories a species of rhetoric. For "good history," as Christopher Shannon has argued, "requires moral judgment [both] in the selection of topics and in the focus of study within each topic."[34] This good judgment that the historian is called to exercise upon the past reposes upon his own moral virtue and is brought to an account by the science of ethics. Surely it is no insult to the historian to be told that the quality of his teaching and writing will be proportionate to the clarity of his perception and the purity of his love for the good. On the contrary, any historian ought to be delighted to be asked to make perfect his will and to nourish his mind with as much wisdom as it can store.

If the good historian is essentially characterized by right judgment, what, then, does he do? He would seem to employ two tools: description (which may include a good deal of analysis) and narrative. In presenting for our consideration examples from the past, the historian can help our understanding in several ways. One is by suggesting, in the example of an individual life, where it is that the mean of virtue lies. To the extent that we do not possess a given virtue, we do not accurately perceive the full implications of its excellence. To investigate and even to analyze in its particulars the generosity of St. Francis, or the magnanimity of St. Louis IX, or the fortitude of Blessed Junipero Serra is to gain a sort of road map toward the virtue in question.[35] Reason can work to correct a defect in our desire for the good, but it must have something upon which to work. Laws, customs, and maxims all provide grist for reason's mill, but, in the end, imitation is usually required as well. And, as living exemplars of the virtues we need are not always at hand or recognizable as such, the historian has a worthy task in describing them.

---

34. See Christopher Shannon, "A Catholic Approach to History," *Catholic Social Science Review* 13 (2008) 9–25.

35. See Robert L. Wilken, "The Lives of the Saints and the Pursuit of Virtue," in *Remembering the Christian Past* (Grand Rapids, MI: Eerdmans, 1995), 121–44.

Historians commonly take interest not only in individual persons, but also in institutions and communities, in practices, customs, and laws. Here, too, the good historian can offer much help to the student of wisdom. For it is one thing to come to an understanding of what the common good is in general, and it is yet another to have the wherewithal to recommend a course of action that will bring our current way of life more closely in accord with the divine order of the universe. Alasdair MacIntyre has argued that we ought to "recognize the existence of . . . the virtue of having an adequate sense of the traditions to which one belongs," and has further suggested that the virtue is a "kind of capacity for judgment" that "manifests itself in a grasp of those future possibilities which the past has made available to the present."[36] Newman not only possessed this virtue to a high degree, he also urged that it be cultivated. "We have a vast inheritance," he wrote, amidst the struggles of the Oxford Movement, "but no inventory of our treasures. All is given us in profusion; it remains for us to catalogue, sort, distribute, select, harmonize, and complete."[37] As it was with Anglican theology in the 1830s, so it is for us today, arguably, with respect to the whole patrimony of Christian civilization. Who among us can claim to have received intact from the past a fully articulated understanding of the kind of social order in which the Christian faith can thrive? Lacking as we do connatural knowledge of right living in Christian community, we rightly look to the past for clues to what it might be. There are, indeed, many signs that our generation will be characterized—much as Newman's was—by its creative reappropriation of the Christian patrimony. But to do that well we need to cultivate this kind of right judgment: Not either idiosyncratically or rigidly, not, as Newman warned, in a "servile imitation of the past," but, as he counseled, with a "reproduction of it as is really new, while it is old."[38] Here, again, Newman writes: "What we need at present for

---

36. Alasdair MacIntyre, *After Virtue: A Study in Moral Theory*, 2nd edition (Notre Dame, IN: University of Notre Dame Press, 1984), 223.

37. *Apologia Pro Vita Sua*, 76.

38. Ibid., 103.

our Church's well-being, is not invention, nor originality, nor sagacity, nor even learning ... at least in the first place, though all gifts of God are in a measure needed, and never can be unseasonable when used religiously, but we need peculiarly a sound judgment, patient thought, discrimination, a comprehensive mind, an abstinence from all private fancies and caprices and personal tastes, —in a word, Divine wisdom."[39]

The subject of judgment naturally leads us to a third characteristic task of the historian: to praise and to blame. Prudent historians, knowing all too well the limits of their knowledge of the past, prefer to keep most of their judgments tentative, even hidden. Yet there are and always will be people and deeds that cannot be described or recounted under the pretense of neutrality. For someone who lived through the twentieth century, an attempt to write a biography of Adolf Hitler that avoided all semblance of negative judgment and blame would be not only unimaginable, it might well seem criminal. One of the marks of a healthy society is that it bestows public honors for virtuous deeds and systematically praises virtuous men and women. In fulfillment of that office, we might indeed find the historian's highest role. What a beautiful achievement it would be if a new school of hagiography—patterned on Newman's Church of the Fathers—were to make the saints of old newly intelligible and attractive to our generation and restore to them the praise that is their due.[40]

Each of these tasks—the describing and analyzing of exemplars, the presentation of aspects of the common good as actually realized in human community, and the praise of the virtuous—is normally accomplished, and generally received, in a narrative mode. Men and women live by story. The stories that we tell ourselves and our children about our own lives, about our local institutions and communities and the larger political communities to which we belong, and

---

39. Ibid., 76.
40. As an example of what a renewed hagiography might resemble, see Robert Louis Wilken, *The Spirit of Early Christian Thought: Seeking the Face of God* (New Haven, CT: Yale University Press, 2003).

especially about our faith, provide us with the context in which we seek the good. At least implicitly, every story we tell about the drama of human existence is situated in the context of a universal history. Good historians, historians whose judgment is rightly informed, have as their essential ofice the custody of that universal narrative, our common memory. In an age of cultural wholeness, the historian is therefore an elder of one kind or another, and the active custody is a positive task of lovingly remembering and handing on that memory. Families, institutions, crafts, and sciences each have their own lore, and that lore needs to be kept in good order for the community to be perpetuated over time—but such tending seems to be different in kind from what academic historians generally spend their time doing and, in fact, rightly the province of the community's older and wiser men and women. The Church and the various levels of political community, in turn, take care of the broader framework of memory by annually reminding the community of its essential turning points through liturgical memorials of the saving acts of God and secular celebrations of the founding and preserving acts of the society.[41]

It is in an age of cultural dislocation and fragmentation that the historian takes on another role, becomes a raider of archives and a wielder of footnotes, and rides out like a knight-errant in defense of wisdom. For, as Newman experienced, it is quite possible for an entire nation to labor under a false narrative, a myth that not only radically alters a part (or even the whole) of the universal narrative, but that also routinely misidentifies the mean where virtue lies, recommends practices and institutions that do not in fact conduce to virtuous living, and, finally, systematically praises and blames the wrong persons and deeds. Faced with this kind of prejudice or false myth—which at times reposes upon centuries of tradition and is celebrated in public festival (e.g., Guy Fawkes Day or Bastille Day)—the historian's task is that of the critic who removes difficulties that stand in the way of the

---

41. See, for instance, the discussion of processions in Augustine Thompson, O.P., *Cities of God: The Religion of the Italian Communes, 1125-1325* (University Park, PA: Pennsylvania State University Press, 2005), 148–60.

persuasive power of the truth. As Newman himself said when engaged in just such an enterprise: "While a community is overrun with prejudices, it is as premature to attempt to prove that doctrine to be true which is the object of them, as it would be to think of building in the aboriginal forest till its trees had been felled."[42]

With all these thoughts in mind, it seems reasonable to conclude that the historian, with his tools of right judgment, has an essential supporting role to play in today's workshop of wisdom. Like all teachers, the historian is called upon to exercise what Benedict XVI has called "intellectual charity."[43] The historian today exercises that charity by removing some of the difficulties that our prejudices and bad habits pose to our reception of the truth. His task is a kind of clearing of the forest, so that the proper liberal arts can more readily accomplish their work of digging the foundations so that the building of the edifice of wisdom might proceed without difficulty. Until we have fully recovered and internalized the intellectual custom of the Church, the historian will have plenty of pagan oaks to smite and gnarled weeds to uproot. And, should we reach that blessed day when our minds are no longer clouded by prejudice, when, that is, the workshop of wisdom can again go about its business knowing that the tradition that supports it is in good order, widely known and loved and carefully tended, then the historian can set aside his footnotes and return to his place at the hearth as an elder and storyteller.

---

42. *Lectures on the Present Position of Catholics in England*, ed. D. M. O'Connell, S.J. (New York: America Press, 1942), v–vi.

43. Benedict XVI, "Address to Catholic Educators," Washington, DC, April 17, 2008.

8

Biology Brought Back to Life

"I WAS OF COURSE right in rejecting most of that biology," Alasdair MacIntyre declares in the prologue to the third edition of *After Virtue*, referring to his well-known doubts about what he had called Aristotle's "metaphysical biology": "If we reject that biology, as we must, is there any way in which [Aristotle's] teleology can be preserved?"[1] It may be asked, however, just how necessary it ever was, or could be, to set aside what is most essential about Aristotle's biology: that he took the whole living organism to be an irreducible starting point for inquiry.[2] Not only has MacIntyre himself profitably reflected upon the flourishing of animals as a way of shedding light on aspects of the human good, but biologists today are once again acknowledging that the whole or-

---

1. Alasdair MacIntyre, *After Virtue: A Study in Moral Theory*, 3rd edition (Notre Dame, IN: University of Notre Dame Press, 2007), xi, 162.

2. A fair *locus classicus* is *De Anima* 2.4.415b13: "in the case of living things, their being is to live," but no less basic is the distinction between the "uniform" and "composite" parts at the outset of the *History of Animals* (1.1.486a5), or the statement of the same point made in terms of organic function in *Parts of Animals* 1.5.645b15-17: "As every instrument and every bodily member is for the sake of something, viz. some action, so the whole body must evidently be for the sake of some complex action." All quotations from Aristotle are taken from *The Complete Works of Aristotle: The Revised Oxford Translation*, ed. Jonathan Barnes, 2 volumes (Princeton: Princeton University Press, 1984).

ganism is an irreplaceable element of their explanations.[3] The present-day conversation among evolutionary biologists, for instance, is considering "evolutionary factors acting on organismal systems' properties," that is upon the whole plant or animal, rather than restricting itself to the genes and their expression.[4] With even Thomas Nagel confessing that he finds materialist reductionism—whether to genes or to atoms—"hard to believe" given the state of contemporary scientific literature, it seems as though a new age of openness to a broadly speaking Aristotelian view of the organism may well be dawning.[5] In light of this development, it seems timely to ask two questions: What might Aristotelians (and other philosophers) have to learn from contemporary biologists? And what might contemporary biologists (and those who take an interest in their work) have to learn from Aristotle?

At first, the answer to both questions seems to be "nothing." Aristotle, after all, held to the fixity of kinds, but we are all evolutionists now. Aristotle was limited to the common experience of the senses, while we have extended our powers of observation by orders of magnitude with our instruments and also in kind through biochemistry. Aristotle's biology, most importantly, was teleological and purposive, while modern biology has been built on the premise of mechanism. Philosophers, moreover, trade in arguments, biologists in observation and experiment. And Philosophers inhabit communities of discourse—both in research and teaching—that do not often overlap with those populated by biologists. Philosophers, finally, are usually

---

3. Although MacIntyre qualifies his *Dependent Rational Animals* (Chicago: Open Court, 1999) as "not an especially Aristotelian" attempt to provide a "biological grounding" for ethical theory, he does consider the organism as a whole as the crucial starting point for reflection (quotations from the prologue to the third edition of *After Virtue*, page xi). For another instance, see his "What Is a Human Body?" in his *The Tasks of Philosophy: Selected Essays*, volume 1 (Cambridge: Cambridge University Press, 2006), 86–103.

4. Massimo Pigliucci and Gerd B. Müller, "Elements of an Extended Evolutionary Synthesis," in *Evolution—The Extended Synthesis*, eds. Pigliucci and Müller (Cambridge, MA: MIT Press, 2010), 13.

5. Thomas Nagel, *Mind and Cosmos: Why the Materialist Neo-Darwinian Conception of Nature Is Almost Certainly False* (New York: Oxford University Press, 2012), 5.

committed to plumbing the ethical consequences of their theories, while biologists generally prefer to keep their science value-free and innocent of consequences other than perhaps technological ones. MacIntyre's caution, then, seems to have been wise. Short of a serious digging down to deeply buried common principles, there seems little prospect that these various causes of division can be healed. Yet it is just such an excavation that now seems possible for the first time in the century and a half since Darwin's *Origin of Species*.

In the attempt, we can take solace from Aristotle's conviction that philosophers had something to learn from physicians—among other empirical students of nature—and that it was incumbent upon the philosopher to labor to draw forth order from the other disciplines and arts.[6] And MacIntyre, surely the most celebrated contemporary Aristotelian, has insisted that we "can *always* ask about the subject matter of our enquiries what characteristics it must have as the kind of subject matter it is . . . if the answers to our questions are to be true answers."[7] We can, therefore, ask about biology what dispositions need to be brought to it in order for it to be prosecuted fruitfully, what will constitute success in biological explanation, and what is the yield or good of biological studies with respect to human life as a whole. Let us ask these Aristotelian questions about the science of life as it is being renewed today.

With Mind and Heart Rightly Tuned[8]

It is the rare scientist who reads deeply in the history of his discipline. Too much concern about the debates of the past distracts from the business at hand, the work that Thomas Kuhn famously called "normal science."[9] In recent years, however, confidence in science

---

6. See *Sense and Sensibilia* 1.436a17-21 and *Metaphysics* 1.2.982a16ff.

7. MacIntyre, "Truth as a Good: A Reflection on *Fides et Ratio*," in his *The Tasks of Philosophy*, 209. Emphasis added.

8. The phrase is taken from John Paul II, *Fides et Ratio*, §48.

9. Thomas S. Kuhn, *The Structure of Scientific Revolutions*, 2nd edition (1962; Chicago: University of Chicago Press, 1970), 23–42.

as a value-neutral, progressive endeavor has been shaken. Scientists themselves now read Kuhn and talk about shifting paradigms. And theoretical biologists have been ransacking libraries to find the works of such hitherto-forgotten biologists as D'Arcy Thompson, William Bateson, and St.-George Mivart.[10] This development is an important one, for the works that are being rediscovered are precisely those that raise questions and difficulties at the level of principles and methods. In other words, they invite the kind of dialectical inquiry that "normal science" is generally proof against. The significance of this new testing of ideas is that an increasing number of biologists are coming to the realization that they have been working within the confines of a tradition of inquiry, a tradition that has limited and directed their attention, their questioning, and their sense of the kind of answers they were seeking—as indeed all traditions do. Biologists are newly aware that they have been trained up into intellectual habits, and they are reflecting critically upon them.

Examples of this kind of reflection are not hard to find. Denis Noble, a physiologist known for his work with heart muscle tissue, finds it puzzling that "we are so fond of the gene-centered view" of the organism, which he considers to be "a magnificent set of blinkers."[11] Franklin Harold, a biochemist, observes that the "single-minded concentration on the relatively tractable problems of chemical structure"—the very sphere of biology's greatest conquests—"has been accompanied by neglect of the higher levels of biological order, often to the point of absurdity."[12] Patrick Bateson, a student of animal behavior, regrets that the terms of engagement in evolutionary theory have long been

---

10. For Thompson, see Franklin M. Harold, *The Way of the Cell: Molecules, Organisms and the Order of Life* (New York: Oxford University Press, 2001), 126–27. For Bateson, see Patrick Bateson, "The Evolution of Evolutionary Theory," *European Review* 18 (2010): 288. For Mivart, see Stephen J. Gould, "Evolution of Organisms," in *The Logic of Life: The Challenge of Integrative Physiology,* eds. C. A. R. Boyd and D. Noble (Oxford: Oxford University Press, 1993), 31, 36.

11. Denis Noble, *The Music of Life: Biology beyond Genes* (Oxford: Oxford University Press, 2006), 4.

12 Harold, *The Way of the Cell,* 31.

set by, on the one hand, the overwhelming emphasis on genes common to what is known as the "Modern Synthesis," and, on the other, a Lamarckian straw man, while, "as so often happens in polarized debates, the excluded middle ground . . . has turned out to be much more interesting and potentially productive than either of the extreme alternatives."[13] Evolutionary theorist Stephen Jay Gould's assessment of the situation was refreshingly crisp: the genetic reductionism of the Modern Synthesis "is effectively dead, despite its persistence as textbook orthodoxy."[14]

These observations about the practice of biology each lay hold of an accidental feature of the science as it is typically pursued. Gene-centered reductionism has had a tremendous power to captivate the imagination, has ridden the coattails of an empirical research program whose successes have won it attention and funding, has succeeded in shaping habits of argumentation, and, finally, has been hallowed with the authority of textbooks. One need not be a social constructivist to affirm that in the dominant tradition of modern biology certain theories have been formed and attitudes shaped less by the nature of living things and more by human invention. It is well, in this connection, to recall Aristotle's admonition that "the effect which lectures produce on a hearer depend upon his habits." "Some people," he observed, "do not listen to a speaker unless he speaks mathematically . . . while others expect him to cite a poet as witness."[15] In the case at hand, the intellectual custom is reductionism, which has become the kind of system that, as Claude Bernard warned long ago, gives the mind "a sort of false confidence and an inflexibility out of harmony with the freedom and suppleness that experimenters should always maintain in their researches."[16]

What is one to do in the face of deficient intellectual custom? Aristotle's prescription was to insist upon proper education: "there-

13. Patrick Bateson, "The Impact of the Organism on Its Descendants," *Genetics Research International*, volume 2012, Article ID 640612.

14. Gould, "Evolution of Organisms," in *The Logic of Life*, 18.

15. *Metaphysics* 2.2.994b32ff.

16. Claude Bernard, *An Introduction to the Study of Experimental Medicine* [1865], trans. H. C. Greene (New York: Dover, 1957), 221.

fore, one must be already trained to know how to take each sort of argument."[17] What is envisioned here is training in the art of logic, but, beyond that, the reflection upon principles and methods that is the properly dialectical part of any discipline. This is, of course, the philosopher's home terrain. Once the second-order reflections begin, philosophy is being committed, no matter who is doing the reflecting.[18] What is at stake is whether the reflection be done well or poorly. It is here that biologists could use a hand from philosophers, for scientists are trained to be critical about method, but typically within fairly narrow parameters. Rules of evidence, such as those governing the use of experimental controls, are rigidly observed. The perception and overthrow of statistical obfuscation is a speciality. Even the use of language can be carefully guarded, at least in the common and at times most appropriate tendency to purge expressions of intentionality from biological explanation.[19] But from the philosopher's vantage, biologists seem deficient with respect to other important tasks of thinking: they do not have a habit of reflecting upon the starting points of our knowing; they are often innocent of the art of defining; they are too prone to be satisfied with metaphor and image.

It seems well to insist that these deficiencies are the manifestations of intellectual custom. Consider Franklin Harold's aspiration for his book, *The Way of the Cell*: "If what I have written here encourages a few readers to look up from their gels and genes to peer at the

---

17. *Metaphysics* 2.2.995a12.

18. For a reflection on philosophy as the natural extension of and complement to the search for truth, see Robert Sokolowski, *Phenomenology of the Human Person* (Cambridge: Cambridge University Press, 2008), 30.

19. For an instance of such careful criticism of one biologist by another, see Mary Jane West-Eberhard, "Dancing with DNA and Flirting with the Ghost of Lamarck," *Biology and Philosophy* 22 (2007): 442: "It does not seem necessary to introduce the concept of 'interpretation' into the discussion of gene action. As in the study of animal communication, it is preferable not to appear to attribute special abilities to organisms but to describe what is actually observed, here, that a particular input or stimulus consistently evokes a particular response, with the response distinctive for different receivers and consistently correlated with the form of the input."

far horizon, I shall be well content."[20] He takes it for granted that the tincture of philosophy has been bleached out of the souls of scientists by their lab duties. Not being accustomed to asking questions about principles and methods, how could they be expected to do so well? Then there is the tendency of modern biology, since its founding in the late nineteenth century, to be dismissive of deeper questions. T. H. Huxley, for instance, asked the question "What is life?" only to set it aside insouciantly: "I, for one, cannot tell you."[21] What biologists would seem likely to profit from is time spent in conversation with some nettlesome Aristotelians. The kind of lesson that I have in mind is like one recently provided by James Barham. Noting that biologists tend to avoid not only the language of intentionality, but even that of agency, he examines a fictitious, but highly credible, circumlocution, of the kind commonly found in biological texts:

> Rather than speak of the bacterium's "pursuing the good," or even "swimming toward its food," why not just speak of its "following a positive attractor gradient"? But notice that this locution is itself a metaphor. After all, bacteria are not "attracted" up a chemical gradient in the same way that iron filings are "attracted" to a magnet.

No, the bacteria move by the work of their own flagella, which is why, as Barham concludes, "the common-sense normative, agential descriptors of bacterial motility . . . are literal," while those employing "physico-chemical terminology" are metaphorical, and they are metaphors that obscure more than they reveal.[22] Arguably there are many biologists today who would profit from just such an occasional visit to a suitably updated *sophronisterion*, wherein they would be forced to hone and sharpen their speech in conversation with captive philoso-

---

20. Harold, *The Way of the Cell*, xii.

21. T. H. Huxley, *Collected Essays* (London: Macmillan, 1894), III:43.

22. James Barham, "Normativity, Agency, and Life," *Studies in History and Philosophy of Biological and Biomedical Sciences* 43 (2012): 99.

phers. Is it too much to suggest that thus constraining philosophers to serve the common good—not to say descend into the cave—could also be an appropriate measure to remind us of our calling?

Beginning with the Organism

If he should listen to the biologists who dissent from the dominant materialist view, what the philosopher will hear is a chorus of praise for the organism. The ability of reductionist and evolutionist research programs to gain funding and thus to multiply investigations has not been without considerable irony: in laboratories and in the field, the whole organism is declaring itself through its superintendence over its parts. Even in a single-celled animal, the subordination of the genes to the organism is manifest. "DNA can do nothing except in a field populated with enzymes," declares one physiologist, while another says "the DNA just sits there, and occasionally the cell reads off from it a sequence that it needs. . . . So the first step in the reductionist chain of cause and effect is not a simple causal event at all."[23] Moreover, the information encoded in the DNA does not suffice to account for the structure of a cell—the placement of its organelles, its shape, and the construction of the cell membrane—so that the DNA clearly stands to the cell as part to whole in a way analogous to the role of the heart or the brain in the human body. Although it is crucial that it be "endowed with a genetic program that ensures the accurate reproduction of all the working parts and is functionally tied into all cellular operations," the cell itself and not its DNA, in Franklin Harold's formulation, is the "dynamic system," that is, the functional whole.[24] This truth has consequences for evolutionary theory as well, as researchers look for experimental confirmation—some would say additional confirmation—of the theory that epigenetic factors of various kinds can spur

---

23. F. Eugene Yates, "Self-Organizing Systems," in *The Logic of Life*, eds. Boyd and Noble, 200; Noble, *The Music of Life*, 7.

24. Harold, *The Way of the Cell*, 96.

evolutionary change.[25] Stephen Jay Gould drew the relevant conclusion, with the help of an apt metaphor, "Organisms are not billiard balls, struck in deterministic fashion by the cue of natural selection and rolling to optimal positions on life's table. They influence their own destiny in interesting, complex, and comprehensible ways. We must," he concluded, "put this concept of organism back into evolutionary biology."[26]

The Aristotelian will take such revelations in stride. The cruder forms of reductionism have always had something unreal about them. Aquinas's observation that the ancient philosophers were "unable to rise above the imagination" in the form taken by their explanations is no less relevant today.[27] Empedocles' man-faced ox-progeny Aristotle thought a mistake just as regrettable as Democritus' theory that the soul was fire: worth arguing against, but not a cause of anxiety. And that is just how we ought to react to the claim that this or that material thing suffices to account for organic activity—whether ours or a bacterium's—and it hardly matters whether the referent is a neuron, a chain of nucleic acids, or a collection of elementary particles. Attempts to explain the integrity and activity of organisms by reference to inert matter "moved" by chance alone, as Aristotle observed, "tell us in reality nothing about nature." The reason for this is plain, as he explained: "the nature of an animal is a first principle."[28] The unity and integrity, that is, the substantial reality of the organism is a starting point for the adventure of our knowing about the world, not something to be established by proof from some prior principle. Our confidence in this fact is absolute in the case of our own bodily selves.

---

25. For an overview, see Bateson, "The Impact of the Organism on Its Descendants."

26. Gould, "Evolution of Organisms," in *The Logic of Life*, eds. Boyd and Noble, 37.

27. *Summa Theologiae* I, Q. 75, Art.1.

28. *Parts of Animals* 1.1.642a16-17. On this point, see the eloquent exposition by Marjorie Grene, *A Portrait of Aristotle* (Chicago: University of Chicago Press, 1963), 135: "To detach efficient from final, or material from formal causes, as many modern biologists profess to do, would be, for Aristotle, to throw the intelligible back into the unintelligible, the principles of things into their mere conditions. It would be to turn knowledge into the vain search for knowledge."

Peter Singer's musings to the contrary notwithstanding, we all know what is the difference between alive and dead, and not only do we prefer the former, we instinctually and vigorously repel even slight attacks upon our persons, let alone attempts to cut us in two. Even horses, as Charles de Koninck pointed out in a classic discussion of the subject of life, are "not indifferent" to the things that can "promote and sustain" them.[29] The hand is no hand once severed from the body, nor is our DNA, the proteins it codes for, or the cells in which it is found capable of independent existence. The parts of living things are just that, parts. Nor can they be accounted for by appeal to the non-living, for neither the elements nor subatomic particles have in them anything more than the potential to be parts of living wholes. The priority of form and actuality to potency and matter remains what it was in Aristotle's day, a truth beyond reasonable doubt.

In the works of such biologists as Franklin Harold and Denis Noble, then, we are in the presence of a shift in intellectual custom, or at least the early stages of one. James Le Fanu, a physician and science writer who stays on top of the latest developments, has suggested that we are on the verge of a new age of post-reductionist science.[30] The hunch seems optimistic. Intellectual habits are hard to break, especially when they are enshrined in custom. Although biochemists "know quite well," according to Harold's testimony, that something essential is lost by grinding up organisms into a protein soup, their "focus on the molecules defines . . . biochemistry" and "undergirds our

---

29. Charles de Koninck, "Is the Word 'Life' Meaningful?," in *Philosophy of Biology*, ed. Vincent E. Smith (New York: St. John's University, 1962), 82. Horses have a way of impressing. See Marjorie Grene, *A Philosophical Testament* (Chicago: Open Court, 1995), 35: "My first ten years farming I found I had lost an ear for the sacred text [*The Critique of Pure Reason*]. We had a great gray Percheron mare named Kitty; I couldn't look at her and ask, was she an appearance or a thing in herself. Of course the question is equally absurd for a gnat or a mouse; but somehow a ton work horse seems more absolutely real, out of all relation, or relativity, to our mode of perception, than smaller critters."

30. James Le Fanu, *Why Us? How Science Rediscovered the Mystery of Ourselves* (New York: Random House, 2009), 253ff.

professional identity."[31] Much closer to the mainstream, therefore, is Nagel's admission that he is "at present unable to conceive" of a cosmology in which life and mind are taken to be starting points rather than epiphenoma of quarks or quantum fields.[32] Mechanistic reductionism, after all, has long had a stronghold on the mind. Even William Paley and his heirs the intelligent design theorists are in a way subject to a version of it. For what they have in common with Descartes is that they take the machine as not merely prior in our understanding, but prior in being to the organism. And it is a great temptation to do so.[33] Aristotle's essential argument that nature acts for an end turns on our understanding of artistic making, which, because we supply the form ourselves, we understand better than the coming-to-be and living of the organisms that we do not make.[34] Yet for having made that argument, Aristotle did not make the mistake of thinking that man-made artifacts were prior in nature or being to organisms.

What does philosophical reflection based on common experience have to offer to contemporary biology?[35] Even if it is little more than the gift of perspective, still it is a significant gift. To know what comes first in our knowing is an essential step toward knowing that we know, that is, to the possession of the knowledge of truth rather than mere

---

31. Harold, *The Way of the Cell*, 34.

32. Nagel, *Mind and Cosmos*, 127.

33. Cf. E. S. Russell, *The Directiveness of Organic Activities* (Cambridge: Cambridge University Press, 1945), 1: "It should be obvious that the analogy of an organism with a machine is superficial and remote, if only for the reason that the organism is a self-maintaining, reproducing and developing unity, and no machine is, or can be, that. But the mechanistic conception is one to which the human mind is peculiarly prone."

34. For a brief and lucid exposition of Aristotle's demonstration that nature acts for an end, see Anthony Andres, "On Finality in Nature," *Second Spring* 15 (2012): 77–81.

35. The essential statements of the status of Aristotle's reflection upon common experience in comparison to modern empirical science are Michael Augros, "Reconciling Science with Natural Philosophy," *The Thomist* 68 (2004): 105–41, and Glen Coughlin's introduction and appendixes to *Aristotle, Physics, or Natural Hearing*, ed. and trans. Coughlin (South Bend: St. Augustine's Press, 2005).

opinion. And to learn that what is being rediscovered—the primacy of the organism—is what many before have known offers biologists a broader sense of intellectual community, which is always healthy and beneficial. The feeling of liberation that the biologist would enjoy from learning that Richard Dawkins and Francis Crick were not the only ones to have thought about life would be akin to that felt by a philosopher who had just discovered that the Churchlands were not the only people to have written about mind. For the biologist to rub shoulders with Edward Stuart Russell, Richard Owen, and William Harvey—to name only three of the most significant Aristotelian biologists of the modern period—to recall their labors with gratitude and to appreciate their intellectual virtues anew: this is a potential for something like the joy the philosopher may experience from stumbling upon Elizabeth Anscombe's pamphlet on Mr. Truman's Degree or Otto Bird's "How to Read an Article of the *Summa*."[36] It is both a source of consolation and a chance to gain a deeper and more reasoned appreciation for what one already held, but had not yet fully thought through.

Beyond these more-or-less strictly biological consolations lies the territory of the soul, a province long ago annexed by philosophers, but perhaps at a cost we ought not to have paid. If, as Aristotle thought, the doctrine of the soul is the proper principle of biological inquiry, then knowledge of it should hardly be withheld from students of cells. Monsignor Robert Sokolowski, for one, has suggested that Catholic higher education would profit from the attempt to revive a "streamlined Thomism" that would "focus on the human soul."[37] And it is interesting to speculate about the complexion of a new generation of biology majors formed in part by the close reading of Aristotle's *Physics* (say, books I-III.3) and *De Anima*, as well as selections from his

---

36. The last-named essay is a model of intellectual charity that deserves to be widely known. Otto Bird, "How to Read an Article of the *Summa*," *New Scholasticism* 27 (1953): 129–59.

37. Robert Sokolowski, "Soul and the Transcendence of the Human Person," in his *Christian Faith and Human Understanding* (Washington, DC: The Catholic University of America Press, 2006), 164. Much of the essay bears on the topic at hand.

biological works, all against the background of the *Nicomachean Ethics* and the *Organon*. For one thing, they would likely make good physicians, because they would understand that health is both the bodily flourishing of the human person and essentially dispositive toward the rational life of the virtues.[38] Yet it seems reasonable to suppose that such a course of studies would bear fruit in biological inquiry as well. Such students would be apt to attend to the whole organism, living in its environment, and looked upon through the lens of the powers of its soul rather than its genetic sequence alone.[39] We could expect advances in the study of the behavior of the higher animals, but also some fruitful speculation about evolutionary theory and its relevance to the classification of plants and animals.[40] Having no great fear of the charge of anthropocentrism, they would be in a good position to transcend the divide between partisans of ecological "integrity" and "ecosystem services"—a divide reminiscent of the once-interminable debates between egoism and altruism. Imagine young biologists able to read de Koninck's *Cosmos* with understanding and equipped to dedicate themselves to empirical studies that might follow out some of the indications made in that astonishing work.[41] Is the prospect utopian? Why should we consider it to be so when it is the biologists themselves who are knocking at our door?

---

38. For two Aristotelian expositions, see Leon R. Kass, M.D., "The End of Medicine and the Pursuit of Health," in his *Toward a More Natural Science: Biology and Human Affairs* (New York: Free Press, 1985), 157–86, and Luke Gormally, "The Good of Health and the Ends of Medicine," in *Natural Law in Contemporary Society*, ed. Holger Zaborowski (Washington, DC: The Catholic University of America Press, 2010), 264–84.

39. Cf. *De Anima* 2.2.413b32-414a1: "Further, some animals possess all these parts of soul, some certain of them only, others one only (this is what enables us to classify animals)."

40. For one broadly Aristotelian overview of the subject of biological classification, see David S. Oderberg, *Real Essentialism* (New York: Routledge, 2007), chapter 9: "Species, biological and metaphysical."

41. For instance, de Koninck would presumably call for the careful study of animal memory. See Charles de Koninck, *The Cosmos*, in *The Writings of Charles de Koninck*, volume 1, ed. and trans. Ralph McInerny (Notre Dame, IN: University of Notre Dame Press, 2008), 298.

Witnesses to the Primacy of Form

One such biologist I was fortunate to have as a teacher, Dr. James Riopel. Although his own laboratory work kept him mostly at the level of cells and molecules, Riopel began his general botany class with the captivating affirmation, "Biology is a liberal art." His imprecision, so characteristic of a scientist reaching beyond his immediate competence, may well elicit a knowing smile from a philosopher, but his spirit should be warmly welcomed. I still remember him pointing up to a tall tree during an outdoor class and telling us that "*Pinus strobus* does well here, but Maine is where its true nobility is to be seen." I doubt that he knew his Aristotle, but it was an echo of Riopel's voice that I heard when I subsequently first read the admonition that "we must not recoil with childish aversion from the examination of the humbler animals, [for] absence of haphazard and conduciveness of everything to an end are to be found in nature's works in the highest degree, and the end for which those works are put together and produced is a form of the beautiful."[42] At their best—which many of them often are—biologists are models of the kind of reverence that the intelligibility of organisms should inspire in us all.

For Franklin Harold, even the lowly *E. coli* is able to provoke wonder. Place a few cells in a beaker with the appropriate nutrients and leave them overnight on an incubator; the next day, "the medium swarms with cells, billions per milliliter, all identical with those of the inoculum. Here, in microcosm," says the biochemist, "is all the mystery of life." There are deep waters here. An organism consisting of a single cell, whose generations are beyond counting, and whose genetic material is so susceptible to change that it may be called "notoriously mutable," has ancestors from 100 million years ago whose DNA testifies to their sameness in kind. "Biological patterns do change over time," says Harold, "but not quickly." And so, even after a hundred years and more of Darwinian controversies, a professional biologist who is a convinced evolutionist remains amazed by

---

42. *Parts of Animals* 1.5.645a15ff.

the spectacle of life's intelligibility: "Why, indeed, are there so many kinds of organisms large and small, and why do they cluster into discrete species?"[43]

This is just the sort of question that philosophers continually ask, and have much to say about in reply. Consider, for instance, Lawrence Dewan's observation that "the popularity of evolution has worked on the *imagination* in the direction of flux schemas which tend to have us overlook the reality of form." Citing an example parallel to Harold's fossilized *E. coli*, Dewan explains that such facts point to "the reality and importance of *stability* in nature," which is a useful reminder because "what we mean by 'form,' after all, is a principle of being, of endurance."[44] The philosopher's gift to the biologist is precisely his reflection upon form as a principle of being, and what flows from that reflection, a steady conviction of the priority of the whole to the part and the form with respect to the matter.[45] The philosopher also has much to offer by way of methodological reflection. For the biologist will from time to time look up from his bench, and say what is on his mind: "The antics of a troop of monkeys in the forest canopy are doubtless consistent with all of physics and chemistry, but this knowledge supplies no insights that will be useful to a student of animal behavior."[46] When the biologist blurts out uncomfortable truths like that one, the philosopher should be ready to point out that the distinction he has just made is as at least as old as the *Phaedo* and is luminously explored in Aristotle's *Parts of Animals*.[47]

What do biologists have to give us in return? The example of their attentiveness to form. Gilbert Highet's tale of how the great Harvard

---

43. Harold, *The Way of the Cell*, 64, 97, 190.

44. Lawrence Dewan, O.P., "Truth and Happiness," *Proceedings of the American Catholic Philosophical Association* 67 (1993): 12. Emphasis in the original. See also his Aquinas Lecture, *St. Thomas and Form as Something Divine in Things* (Milwaukee: Marquette University Press, 2007).

45. See, in this connection, *Metaphysics* 12.3.1070a19-21, and for a careful presentation of the relevant arguments, see John Goyette, "St. Thomas on the Unity of Substantial Form," *Nova et Vetera*, English edition 7 (2009): 781–90.

46. Harold, *The Way of the Cell*, 218.

47. See *Phaedo* 99B, and *Parts of Animals* 1.1.642a1ff.

anatomist Louis Agassiz "trained his laboratory pupils to see" is justly famous. He began with a passage from a student's memoir. "Agassiz brought me a small fish," wrote the apprentice,

> placing it before me with the rather stern requirement that I should study it, but should on no account talk to anyone concerning it, nor read anything relating to fishes, until I had his permission to do so. To my inquiry "What shall I do?" he said in effect: "Find out what you can without damaging the specimen; when I think that you have done your work I will question you." Neither the first day's work nor the first week's satisfied the master. A second week of ten-hour days was what the student needed to make the necessary gains. Highet's commentary was apt: "Admirable, this training. No one who had gone through it could ever forget that the scientist's duty is to observe."[48]

It is well for us philosophers to be reminded, from whatever quarter the reminder may come, that "the proper object of the human mind is whatness or nature existing in material bodies."[49] Or of the corollary that our learning naturally proceeds "through that which is less intelligible by nature to that which is more intelligible . . . [and that] it is our work to start from what is more intelligible to oneself and make what is intelligible by nature intelligible to oneself." This is the reason why the one we call *the* Philosopher taught us that "we must look first" at "substances among sensible things."[50] The opposing danger today does not so much seem to be premature flights of metaphysical speculation—although that has indeed been a concern in the past and may be so again—but rather that we will not much look at sensible substances at all, preferring to them the writings of our fellow philosophers.[51] The danger, then, is that we will not show forth

---

48. Gilbert Highet, *The Art of Teaching* (New York: Vintage, 1955), 214–15.

49. *Summa Theologiae* I, Q. 84. Art. 7.

50. *Metaphysics* 7.3.1029b2ff.

51. Cf. Jude P. Dougherty, *The Nature of Scientific Explanation* (Washington, DC: The Catholic University of America Press, 2013): xvi: "Today philosophy has become

in our own philosophical lives what Aristotle identified as one of the marks of philosophy, when he explained that "dialectic is merely critical, while philosophy claims to know."[52] I do not mean to suggest that we are today deficient in our understanding of the primacy of natural form, either within Aristotle's philosophy or in our life of knowing.[53] Rather, it is our habits of knowing that may not have caught up with our convictions.

The most popular outdoor activities in contemporary culture, and by a wide margin, are gardening and the feeding and watching of birds: just the sort of activities to which people are drawn by the intelligible beauty of the forms of living things. To recognize the first swelling buds of spring as belonging to the red maple and the soft, sweet warbling whistle in the graveyard as the bluebird's call is to be consoled and to feel more at home in the world. We are made richer for our contact with the being of living things, because, as St. John Paul II put it, "all that is the object of our knowledge becomes a part of our life."[54] What, then, is the prospect of a biology renewed by the understanding that "in the case of living things, their being is to live"?[55]

---

so specialized that . . . it has . . . resulted in a kind of trivialization that permits whole careers to be spent on isolated problems in the work of a single philosopher of little consequence, or worse still, on the youthful efforts of a philosopher whose mature works repudiated his early efforts."

52. *Metaphysics* 4.2.1004b25.

53. Aristotelian scholarship now commonly recognizes the important role played by biology in Aristotle's thinking and teaching. For an overview of the recent literature, see Sophia M. Connell, "Toward an Integrated Approach to Aristotle as a Biological Philosopher," *Review of Metaphysics* 55 (2001): 297–322; and for an example of just such an integrated approach, see Christopher V. Mirus, "Order and the Determinate: The Good as a Metaphysical Concept in Aristotle," *Review of Metaphysics* 65 (2012): 499–523.

54. *Fides et Ratio*, §1. And see Dewan, "Truth and Happiness," 14: "Things lower than man are not merely 'survivors,' 'existence machines.' As each having a form, as each revealing 'the light of mind,' they are intrinsically good; and as fitting in in the universal order, they have an even higher mode of goodness and being. Things lower than man have a further value insofar as we humans have a mind which comes to a vision of ourselves and God through such things."

55. *De Anima* 2.4.415b13.

That biologists will trade in their cramped and narrow vision for a broad and liberating one, and we philosophers will grease our boots, pick up our walking sticks, and join our biologist friends as exemplars of attentiveness to form.

9

Newman's Collegiate Ideal

TO NEWMAN, SHE WAS "the glory of the middle ages"; to Pope Gregory IX, who may be counted among her founders, she was the *officina sapientiae*, "wisdom's workshop."[1] She was built by the opposing geniuses of Abelard and Hugh of St. Victor, provided a home to Aquinas and Robert de Sorbon, and, in her colleges, nourished Erasmus and Calvin, Loyola and Bossuet. The University of Paris, hardly recognizable today thanks to Bonaparte's decrees, is surely the archetypal institution of higher learning in the West. Her story, like that of Western education as a whole, is one of heroes and villains, moments of discovery and fruitful innovation, times of sterile debate, and outbursts of iconoclasm. She was founded for the sake of wisdom, but she has been transformed into an institution her founders would not recognize. The University of Paris today is no different from the universities of Berlin, London, or Virginia; she exists to fulfill the Enlightenment's project of rational autonomy and mastery of nature. Christian wisdom, that pure and peaceable wisdom that is "from above" (Jas 3:17) wanders now in exile. May it not be the task of our generation to find for her a new home? A model for the kind of institution in

---

1. John Henry Newman, *The Idea of a University*, ed. Martin J. Svaglic (Notre Dame, IN: University of Notre Dame Press, 1982), 13. Gregory IX, *Parens scientiarum* [1231], in Heinrich Denifle, O.P., *Chartularium Universitatis Parisiensis*, I (Paris, 1899; Bruxelles: Culture et Civilisation, 1964), 137.

which wisdom can flourish is to be found in the educational writings of Blessed John Henry Newman, indeed, even within his *Idea of a University*, so often seen as a kind of charter for the modern university, but so often read only in part and in isolation from its author's deepest convictions. For Newman's ideal was not so much the university itself as it was the "University seated and living in Colleges."[2] The college he held to be not a place for advanced but for elementary studies; not an academy of savants and researchers, but an alma mater inhabited by teachers who embraced their vocation's pastoral role; not a chance collection of individuals building their careers, but a kind of fellowship, even a friendship, whose characteristic activity was to "rejoice in the truth" (cf. 1 Cor. 13:6). Overlooked by most commentators, or mentioned only to be dismissed, Newman's collegiate ideal nevertheless holds considerable promise for our time.

Elementary Studies

Newman's exposition of his collegiate ideal is contained in his essays on the *Rise and Progress of Universities*, written as a companion to the *Discourses on University Teaching* with which he had opened his tenure as rector of the Catholic University in Dublin from 1851 to 1858. Running through the essays is a distinction between the "essence" of university education, on the one hand, and what the university requires for its "integrity," on the other. The former consists in "influence," the latter in "law." The "university principle" is the search for truth, according to which the charismatic professor gains students on the strength of his reputation for learning. Abelard's magnetic genius served as Newman's example of the principle, showing its "power to collect students" but also its "impotence to preserve and edify them." The university is founded upon personal virtue, or, virtue failing, at least personal attractiveness. The college, conversely, is less attractive, but it is as solid as the ivy-covered stones of its walls. Universities

---

2. John Henry Newman, *Rise and Progress of Universities* [1854], in *Historical Sketches*, vol. III (London: Longmans, 1894), 229.

are staffed by professors, colleges by tutors. The college is a "household" that "offers an abode to its members, and requires or involves the same virtuous and paternal discipline which is proper to a family and home." And while the university trades in brilliance and discovery, the college carefully hands on what is already known: "it is the school of elementary studies, not of advanced."[3]

In his conception of "elementary studies" lies the heart of Newman's educational theory. This fact has not been often enough acknowledged, in part because his convictions so radically disagree with the practices of our age, but also because the essays in which he explained his views have been overshadowed by the sparkling rhetoric of the nine *Discourses on University Teaching* that form the body of the *Idea of a University*. While the *Discourses* accord with his collegiate ideal, they only advert in passing to the need for elementary studies. His substantial treatment of them is found in two essays published in a volume on *University Subjects* in 1858, and, since 1873, as appendixes to the *Idea of a University*, one on "Elementary Studies" and another called "Discipline of Mind." Together with his *Rise and Progress of Universities*, these two essays are the hidden gems of Newman's educational theory, so hidden, in fact as even to have been omitted from the most recent edition of the *Idea of a University*.[4]

It is well to begin with "Discipline of Mind," which Newman delivered as a sort of admonition to the adult auditors of the Dublin University's evening lecture series. The address echoed the themes of his earlier work "The Tamworth Reading Room," a series of letters to the London *Times* in which he had criticized Bentham's view of knowledge and moral education. As in the Tamworth letters, here he lashed out at his contemporaries, railing against the "barren mockery of knowledge" offered by newspapers, journals, and lectures. Yet

---

3. *Rise and Progress of Universities*, 77, 192, 214–15.

4. See Frank M. Turner, ed., *The Idea of a University* (New Haven: Yale University Press, 1996). The editor explains his choice at ix-x. It should be noted that in his own comments on the text (301), Professor Turner affirmed the need for "scholar-teachers" who "value the ordinarily extraordinary achievement of teaching students to think critically, to speak articulately, and to write clearly."

unlike the Tamworth letters, which sought to defend Christianity against secular liberalism, the Dublin address targeted shoddy thinking rather than unbelief. Against the mere vulgarization of knowledge, he championed a conception of the "formation of mind" to be accomplished by "methodical and laborious teaching."[5] In his sixth *Discourse*, he had identified the "practical error of the last twenty years" as the "distracting and enfeebling [of] the mind by an unmeaning profusion of subjects."[6] His concern was not limited to formal studies; he asked "what permanent advantage the mind gets" by the "desultory reading" of journals and popular accounts of the sciences, plainly implying that the answer was none at all. He warned of the danger of reading or of attending lectures from "mere curiosity" and insisted that his auditors "carefully distinguish . . . between the mere diversion of mind and its real education." Brilliant lectures and even wide reading do not bring about the mind's improvement. That end could be achieved only by the persistent effort of the learner whose "mind must go half-way to meet what comes to it from without," coupled with a particular kind of teaching, a "catechetical instruction, which consists in a sort of conversation between your lecturer and you."[7] For Newman, discipline of mind reposed upon a conscious and decisive act of the will: "We must make up our minds to be ignorant of much, if we would know anything."[8]

The long essay on "Elementary Studies" sheds further light on Newman's conception of a well-formed mind. He sketched contrasting portraits of a well-prepared student and a poorly prepared one as they took their entrance examinations for the university. The poor student, Mr. Brown, was a "youth of inaccurate mind," who rejoiced "to profess all the classics, and to learn none of them." He was widely read in classical texts and historical studies, but, upon examination

---

5. "Discipline of Mind: An Address to the Evening Classes," in *Idea of a University*, 377, 378, 376.

6. *Idea of a University*, 107.

7. "Discipline of Mind," 367, 371, 368.

8. "The Tamworth Reading Room," in *Discussions and Arguments on Various Subjects*, new impression (London: Longmans, 1899), 280.

was found to have retained almost nothing from his reading. Newman wrote four pages of an imaginary entrance examination in which Mr. Brown proved himself not only ignorant, but unaware of and unconcerned by his ignorance. In marked contrast, Mr. Black, the good student, possessed, at the age of eighteen, a carefully honed skill in the classical languages. The four pages of his dialogue with the examiner make painful reading today, so deft are his answers and so difficult are the questions he is posed; the example suggests that Newman would be likely to regard most American professors today to be half-educated, to say nothing of our students. For Newman held the essential foundation of real education to consist in grammar, by which he meant "the structure and characteristics of the Latin and Greek languages," leading to an ability not only to read and to analyze the languages, but also to compose in them.[9]

Newman did not often speak of grammar in the *Discourses on University Teaching*, but what he said in the preface to them was plain enough: "I hold very strongly that the first step in intellectual training is to impress upon a boy's mind the idea of science, method, order, principle, and system; of rule and exception, of richness and harmony. This is commonly and excellently done by making him begin with Grammar."[10] He insisted upon depth, not breadth, and the deep and solid foundation was to be laid in the line-by-line study of classical texts. Such study he held to be the proper province of the college, as opposed to the university. Even at its origins in the thirteenth century, the university had preferred the work of discovery and disputation to that of the slow and painful formation of the mind of students. For all of his reverence for the glories of the University of Paris, Newman sided with the "champions of the ancient learning" from the cathedral schools that it had supplanted:

> We find them complaining that the careful "getting up," as we now call it, "of books," was growing out of fashion. Youths

---

9. "Elementary Studies," in Svaglic, ed., *Idea of a University*, 250.
10. *Idea of a University*, xliv.

once studied critically the text of poets or philosophers; they got them by heart; they analyzed their arguments; they noted down their fallacies; they were closely examined in the matters which had been brought before them in lecture; they composed. But now, another teaching was coming in; students were promised truth in a nutshell; they intended to get possession of the sum-total of philosophy in less than two or three years; and facts were apprehended, not in their substance and details, by means of living and, as it were, personal documents, but in dead abstracts and tables.[11]

In painting this contrast, Newman placed himself within an older tradition of education formed by, among others, Hugh of St. Victor and St. Augustine. "The way to make progress" in learning, real progress toward "accuracy of mind," he contended, making use of a traditional metaphor, was "not to swallow knowledge" but "to masticate and digest it."[12] Only careful exercise and discipline could prepare the mind for the advanced studies that Newman envisioned in his *Discourses*. And such exercises are at home in the college, which is a "place of training for those who are not only ignorant, but have not yet learned how to learn, and who have to be taught, by careful individual trial, how to set about profiting by the lessons of a teacher."[13]

Newman's own education consisted in just such elementary studies. He began Latin and Greek in his tenth year, and by the age of fourteen had proceeded to Herodotus and to the stage acting of Latin plays.[14] His friend and Oxford contemporary Isaac Williams had a similar education, and once testified that "I was so used to think in Latin that when I had to write an English theme . . . I had to trans-

---

11. *Rise and Progress of Universities*, 198.

12. Newman, "Elementary Studies," 231. See *The Didascalicon of Hugh of St. Victor: A Medieval Guide to the Arts*, trans. Jerome Taylor (New York: Columbia University Press, 1961), 94 and 214n59.

13. *Rise and Progress of Universities*, 214–15.

14. A. Dwight Culler, *The Imperial Intellect: A Study of Newman's Educational Ideal* (New Haven: Yale University Press, 1955), 2–3.

late my ideas, which ran in Latin, into English."[15] Whether Newman thought and prayed more in Latin or Greek than in English is an open question, but his own Latin studies at Oxford were so advanced that his challenge was not to understand the language or even to master its authors, but to perfect his own style in original Latin composition. When he became a Fellow of Oriel, he found mentors who taught him that the foundation of any real education lay in just such elementary studies as grammar and logic. From Edward Copleston, Edward Hawkins, and Richard Whately, he gained the conviction that education was essentially a "discipline in accuracy of mind," a conviction he retained for life.[16] For whereas his *Apologia Pro Vita Sua* may be read—at least in its early chapters—as the story of his movement away from his Oriel mentors, in the *Discourses* he cited them frequently and with approval, and when it came time to dispel the Benthamite misconception of education, he stepped aside and allowed Copleston to speak for him in a lengthy quotation. Newman's fidelity to the Oriel School's ideal of education was absolute: "Many changes has my mind gone through: here it has known no variation or vacillation of opinion."[17]

The Oriel dons, for all their theological liberalism, belonged to an older educational tradition that dissented from the Enlightenment's quest for encyclopedic knowledge. Copleston, the provost of Oriel, had been responsible for opening up the Oriel Fellowship by the competitive examination of men of talent, irrespective of their birth or connections. This Oriel examination, to R. W. Church's mind, "was altogether a trial, not of how much men knew, but of *how* they knew"; or, as Newman said, it "tested what you were rather than what you knew."[18] Like all his Oriel colleagues, Copleston held for depth rather than for breadth, as suggested by his chosen device, the an-

---

15. R. W. Church, *The Oxford Movement: Twelve Years, 1833–1845*, ed. Geoffrey Best (Chicago: University of Chicago Press, 1970), 51.

16. "Elementary Studies," 248.

17. *Idea of a University*, 3.

18. Culler, *Imperial Intellect*, 26, 29.

cient adage *Multum, non multa.*[19] "The more I think on it," Copleston
once wrote to a friend, "the more am I convinced that to exercise the
mind of the student is the business of education, rather than to pour in
knowledge."[20] Of the Oriel Fellows, Edward Hawkins was the first to
set to work forging the fine metal of Newman's mind. Newman began
to grow apart from Hawkins as early as 1828, but remained forever
grateful to him, testifying that Hawkins had "taught me to weigh my
words, and to be cautious in my statements" and had "led me to that
mode of limiting and clearing my sense in discussion."[21] Hawkins having tempered the metal, it fell to Richard Whately to shape it. In Newman's words, Whately "taught me to think and to use my reason."[22] He
did so by insisting that education be an apprenticeship to the mind
and the method of Aristotle.

That John Henry Newman's mind was formed by the study and
teaching of Aristotle's *Nicomachean Ethics* has been insufficiently acknowledged. Consider, from the heart of the *Discourses*, Newman's
pledge of loyalty to the "oracle of nature and of truth": "While we
are men, we cannot help, to a great extent, being Aristotelians, for
the great Master does but analyze the thoughts, feelings, views, and
opinions of human kind. He has told us the meaning of our own words
and ideas, before we were born. In many subject matters, to think correctly, is to think like Aristotle."[23] Then there is Newman's admission
that he was "taught to think" by Oxford's foremost Aristotelian, Richard Whately. He was devoted to the *Ethics* and the *Rhetoric*, but also to
Aristotle's logical works, and his conception of "elementary" education
was similar to Aristotle's doctrine of *paideia*, the general acquaintance
with the method and principles of the various sciences that enables
an auditor rightly to judge a discourse on any topic. Thus Whately

---

19. Ibid, 38. Literally "much, not many."

20. Ibid.

21. John Henry Newman, *Apologia Pro Vita Sua*, ed. Ian Ker (London: Penguin, 1994),
    29.

22. Ibid., 31.

23. *Idea of a University*, 82-3.

insisted upon the distinction between "elementary" and "superficial" knowledge, the latter being more "showy" and more "practically useful," but the former being more "philosophical."[24] When Newman, in turn, decided to write about the perfection of the mind, he followed Whately closely. He warned that "memory can tyrannize" and that "it is no great gain to the intellect to have enlarged the memory at the expense of faculties which are indisputably higher." Specialized studies, whether historical, literary, or scientific, risk flooding the mind with myriad particulars without imparting any essential discipline: "knowledge, in proportion as it tends more and more to be particular, ceases to be Knowledge." The truly educated mind is not a well-ordered storehouse with carefully stacked shelves, but a lens, a tool for seeing, that "discerns the end in every beginning." Newman's ideal was a mind capable of reflecting upon its own knowledge: "If we would improve the intellect, first of all, we must ascend; we cannot gain real knowledge on a level; we must generalize, we must reduce to method, we must have a grasp of principles."[25]

As a teacher, Newman placed his students under Aristotle's tutelage, especially through the careful study of the Greek text of the *Ethics*. As evidence, there are the study questions that he sent to his pupil Henry Wilberforce in January 1830: "How does A. obtain his definition of happiness—and mention the specific use of each chapter previous to it, and how it comes in." "What is the connection between orthos logos and taste, and where does A. allude to the connection?" "How are habits of virtue proved to be voluntary?" "The traces of discoverable in A's treatise that he made the principle of virtue extend to the minutiae of conduct."[26] The questions are impressive, but, one might argue, resemble those that any thorough teacher would ask. Yet Newman's carefully annotated copy of the *Ethics* and his accompany-

---

24. Whately, quoted in Culler, *Imperial Intellect*, 202.

25. *Idea of a University*, 85, 104–7.

26. Newman to Henry Wilberforce, January 18, 1830, in *Letters and Diaries of John Henry Newman*, volume 2, ed. Ian Ker and Thomas Gornall, S.J. (Oxford: Clarendon Press, 1979), 189–90.

ing notes revealed to Dwight Culler, who made a close study of them, that he had insisted not merely on knowledge of the text, but on submission to its doctrine: "Newman's whole effort . . . was not merely to bring out what Aristotle had said but, by means of what he had said, to bring home to the student the real nature of justice."[27] Furthermore, Newman affirmed in the *Discourses* that the subjects of study and texts should be considered "not only as regards the attainment of truth . . . but as regards the influence which they exercise upon those whose education consists in the study of them."[28] To read Aristotle with care is to gain what Newman called "discipline of mind," because Aristotle immediately directs his discussions toward the elucidation of reliable principles and then proceeds with great care, and generally by syllogisms, to his appointed conclusions. What is more, the tone of the *Nicomachean Ethics* is one of high seriousness. In fact, one of Newman's contemporaries at Oxford, Frederick Oakeley, went so far as partially to credit the Oxford Movement to the common reading of the text, which had done so much to "form [the] character and regulate [the] tone" of Oxford studies.[29]

What would it mean to base an education upon the study of the classics and apprenticeship to Aristotle? Such an attempt would represent the choice of depth over breadth and would make restraint the leading characteristic of the curriculum. Newman, it seems, would approve. In his first official sermon from the university pulpit, given in 1826 when he was fully under the influence of Copleston, Hawkins, and Whately, he affirmed their line: "It is by tedious discipline that the mind is taught to overcome those baser principles which impede it in philosophical investigations, and to moderate those nobler faculties and feelings which are prejudicial when in excess."[30] The institution

---

27. Culler, *Imperial Intellect*, 78–79.

28. *Idea of a University*, 75.

29. Frederick Oakeley, "Historical Notes of the Tractarian Movement," *Dublin Review*, new series 1 (1863): 180–81.

30. Newman, "The Philosophical Temper, First Enjoined by the Gospel," in *Fifteen Sermons Preached before the University of Oxford* [1843], new impression (London: Longmans, 1900), 9.

that is the proper home for such a discipline of mind is a college composed of teachers dedicated to elementary studies. Such an institution
can only be sustained by a devotion to the task of forming students.

The Pastoral Office of the Tutor

"To discover and to teach are distinct functions," Newman wrote in
the preface to the Discourses, "they are also distinct gifts, and are not
commonly found united in the same person."[31] Nor, he might well
have added, do they belong to the same institutional setting or professional role. Indeed, his collegiate ideal calls for a particular kind of
teacher as much as it does for a particular kind of studies. Just as collegiate studies were to be exercises for the mind, so also the collegiate
teacher was a kind of drill instructor, whose motto should be "a little,
but well," and who showed his commitment to his craft by continuing
to return to those same subjects he had long ago mastered, but kept
alive in order to hand on effectively.[32] Thus Newman himself studied
Greek drama and Aristotle more diligently when a tutor and examiner than he had as a student, reading so many hours a day that he fell
ill from overexertion during the examination season at the end of the
Michaelmas term of 1827.[33] The collegiate teacher, then, was a tutor,
not a professor.[34] He was an apprentice to a tradition and to a body
of texts, not an autonomous master teaching his own doctrine. And,
what is more, the tutor was, in Newman's conception, not only or even
principally a teacher; he was a paternal authority making the college
to be all "which is implied in the name of home."[35]

Newman's convictions about the paternal role of the college tutor may be perceived in his own practice as a tutor at Oriel from 1826

---

31. *Idea of a University*, xl.
32. "Elementary Studies," 251.
33. See the discussion in Culler, *Imperial Intellect*, 58.
34. See Michael Keating, "Professors versus Tutors: Pusey and Vaughan at Oxford,"
    Newman Studies Journal 7 (2010): 55–74.
35. *Rise and Progress of Universities*, 214.

through 1830. This period in his life has been described by many, beginning with Newman himself, who left behind fragments of an autobiography that discussed those years.[36] Oriel College then kept four tutors for its sixty or so undergraduates; Newman was the most junior of the four when he began his tenure, having been chosen by the provost, Copleston, on account of his earnestness. The prior year he had assisted Whately at St. Alban's Hall, a boarding house for students unable to gain admission to one of the regular colleges, and he had shown considerable pluck in dealing with the rowdy drinkers who were its denizens. He had from his youth been serious-minded and zealous in his observance of the Christian faith, but the year at St. Alban's coupled with the reception of Holy Orders seems to have given a determined direction to his fervor. In his first months as tutor he penned a prayer in his diary that he might take up his duties "remembering I am a minister of God" with the "commission to preach the Gospel," and that "I shall have to answer for the opportunities given me of benefitting those who are under my care."[37] And whether it was from a touch of scruples, or whether it was really the case that he was tempted to pursue his own interests rather than to attend to his pupils, he wrote to his sister in March 1826 of the "danger of the love of literary pursuits assuming too prominent a place in the thoughts of a College Tutor, or his viewing his situation merely as a secular office."[38]

Newman conceived of the tutor's role as a pastoral one, involving, as he would later put it, "the care of souls."[39] Such a view was foreign to his Oriel mentors, and particularly to Whately, the very model of donnish eccentricity, who may have been the original for Newman's comment that he had known teachers who were "cut off

---

36. See John Henry Newman, *Autobiographical Writings*, ed. Henry Tristram (New York: Sheed and Ward, 1957).

37. Culler, *Imperial Intellect*, 52.

38. *Letters and Diaries of John Henry Newman*, vol. 1, eds. Ker and Gornall, S.J. (Oxford: Clarendon Press, 1978), 280–81.

39. Culler, *Imperial Intellect*, 40.

from the taught as by an insurmountable barrier."[40] In fact, Newman's ministerial conception of the teacher's role was closer to the convictions of another Fellow of Oriel, John Keble, who was not a member of the school of Copleston and Whately because much more conservative in his theological and political convictions. It was, therefore, an auspicious occasion when, in 1828, Newman was joined in the ranks of the Oriel tutors by two of Keble's disciples, Robert Wilberforce and Hurrell Froude.

The story of Newman's friendship with Froude, Wilberforce, and Keble belongs to the history of the Oxford Movement and has been told often and eloquently. Our concern is not with what the episode meant for Newman's spiritual odyssey, but with the high ideal that the three young teachers shared and attempted to put into practice.[41] The system of tuition that they inherited was little short of disorganized. Students could begin their studies in any of the three terms and were thrown into lectures irrespective of teachers. If a student desired close coaching for the honors examination, he would not study with his tutor, but instead contract with an outside, private instructor and devote his summer vacation to strenuous reading. The moral formation of students was left to exhortations from the pulpit and to the minimal standards of decorum enforced by university rules. Newman and his colleagues initiated a reform of the system; they had each student placed under the direct authority of one or another tutor who would prepare him for the honors examination and also exercise a salutary authority over his moral development. As the sixty undergraduates were too many and too various in aptitude and disposition for the new system to apply to all of them, only a subset received this careful, personal tuition—and then only in selected subjects such as moral philosophy and divinity—while the others, largely the "gentleman commoners" who were known for their social standing and their drinking more than for their studies, would continue to take the larger classes taught to all of the students together.

---

40. *Rise and Progress of Universities*, 75.

41. See Culler, *Imperial Intellect*, 46–79.

Opposition to these reforms soon arose, however, from the new Provost of Oriel, Hawkins, who preferred the older model and may have been suspicious of Newman's growing influence over his students. After several months of querulous exchanges, Hawkins forced Newman and his friends out of teaching by the administrative measure of denying them further students, and so the experiment came to an end in 1831.

The first of Newman's many biographers, Wilfrid Ward, supposed that had Newman's tenure as tutor not come to an end, the Oxford Movement would never have begun, for lack of opportunity.[42] Newman's approach to the office of tutor, after all, had made it into a most absorbing task. Thus in June 1829, after six months of the new system, Newman admitted to his sister Harriett, "I am so hungry for Irenaeus and Cyprian—I long for the Vacation." Yet halfway through that same vacation he told Froude that his dream to spend long hours reading the Fathers had not been realized: "as to the Fathers . . . I must in time give up the tuition, and be a gentleman, or rather a fellow."[43] Newman knew from experience that the tutor's duty to pass on elementary knowledge required that he restrain himself from those scholarly pursuits he might prefer and instead devote himself to the subjects most necessary to his charges. Similarly, when Robert Wilberforce began his tenure as tutor, he had to set aside his studies of Hebrew in favor of the Greek tragedies. He found the transition taxing, lamenting to Froude "how little I know on the subjects I lecture about."[44] In addition to their classical studies, all three of the tutors were also working through the mathematical texts studied by their students, with Froude even writing a pamphlet calling for the return to Euclid, and Newman devoting himself to an extensive study of more recent mathematical treatises.[45]

---

42. Ward, quoted in David Newsome, *The Parting of Friends: The Wilberforces and Henry Manning* (Grand Rapids: Eerdmans, 1993 [1966]), 95.

43. *Letters and Diaries of John Henry Newman*, 2:150 and 158.

44. Newsome, *Parting of Friends*, 84.

45. See Culler, *Imperial Intellect*, 80–81.

Ward's contention, while doubtless true in part, obscures the fact that the Tractarian principles would not likely have enjoyed such a wide influence if Newman had not first collected around himself what his student Tom Mozley called "as devoted a body of pupils as Oxford had ever seen."[46] Like his contemporary John Bosco, the tireless educator of the orphans of Turin, Newman was seen everywhere with his charges, proving by his practice the truth of his theory that "personal influence" was the "means of propagating the truth."[47] He ate with his students, walked and rode with them, taught them formally and through hours of informal discussion, and, perhaps most importantly, led them in worship and preached to them. "None of those who remember them can adequately estimate the effect of Mr. Newman's four o'clock sermons at St. Mary's," wrote R. W. Church, who had heard them as a student; "they made men think of the things which the preacher spoke of, and not of the sermon or the preacher."[48] To Frederick Oakeley, who also attended Newman's services, even his reading of the Bible was "a sermon in which you forgot the human preacher; a drama in which the vividness of the representation was marred by no effort and degraded by no art."[49] The religious character of collegiate education, to Newman, was not guaranteed by the teaching of theology as one subject among many or even by the presence of a chapel on the grounds; it was secured by an atmosphere of holiness penetrating every aspect of collegiate life and nourished by teachers who had devoted themselves to the pursuit of Christian wisdom.

Rejoicing in the Truth

That Newman held a collegiate education to consist in elementary studies taught by tutors fulfilling an essentially paternal role is plain,

---

46. Quoted in Culler, *Imperial Intellect*, 67.
47. See Newman's fourth University Sermon, "Personal Influence, the Means of Propagating the Truth," (1832), and his *Autobiographical Writings*, 90.
48. Church, *Oxford Movement*, 92–93.
49. Oakeley, "Historical Notes of the Tractarian Movement," 186.

for he addressed the points directly. The third and crucial characteristic of his collegiate ideal is more elusive because he seems, at least in part, to have taken it for granted. So it often is with talents; one becomes accustomed to exercising them and forgets their rarity and price. Among Newman's many gifts, two stand out for their connection to the life of teaching: his quenchless desire for truth and the generosity with which he devoted himself to friendship. His own device, *Cor ad cor loquitur*, heart speaking to heart, may be understood as the combination of these two characteristics. Indeed, Newman, the great modern authority on Christian education, agreed with St. Augustine that the purest source of happiness was a *gaudium de veritate*, joy in the truth, and that true Christian friendship consisted in the sharing of that joy.[50]

It was the Oriel common room that first transformed Newman from an introspective and somewhat brooding young man into not merely a well-functioning member of a community, but a leader and a fount of friendship. At Oriel, Newman was granted a seat at a table known for brilliant and congenial, if at times disputatious conversation. He later credited the "atmosphere of the Oriel Common Room" with having shaped his theological convictions and having given him a sense of the church beyond what his evangelical upbringing had provided. What is remarkable about his account of Oriel is that he signals the "unity" and "unanimity" of the Fellows. Copleston, Whately, and the others loved the mutual pursuit of truth and were "proud of their College" because they held in common an "exceptional strictness" of discipline and seriousness of mind.[51] The Oriel School was not, however, of a cast of mind that could hold Newman's allegiance permanently. As his religious practice steadily deepened during his years as tutor, he came to belong to an emerging party identified with Keble and E. B. Pusey, a party that soon crystallized around the friendship between Newman and Hurrell Froude.

The history of that party, whether told by Newman himself in

---

50. See Augustine, *Confessions*, X.xxiii.20.

51. *Autobiographical Memoirs*, 73.

his *Apologia Pro Vita Sua* or by its many stirring narrators since, may be the most compelling story of the friendship of ardent seekers after the truth since the eighth and ninth books of Augustine's *Confessions*.[52] As the Oxford Movement drew to its close in the autumn of 1843, when Newman resigned his living in the Church of England, he preached his final sermon as an Anglican on "The Parting of Friends." Even among Newman's sermons, this one stands out. He told of the sorrowful partings related in sacred history: of St. Paul from his followers, of David from Jonathan, of Orpah from Naomi, of the Son of Man from his disciples. Newman's closing plaint began by addressing his own circle of friends, "O my brethren, O kind and affectionate hearts, O loving friends," and ended by pleading for their prayers.[53] The signs of a parting of the ways were correctly read by Newman in 1843; in later years, one by one the members of his fellowship went each his own way, until Newman was left only with one close friend, Ambrose St. John. In comparison to his two decades and more at Oxford, the long years as a Roman Catholic seem worn and melancholy.

Newman's formative years at Oriel, his years as tutor and dean, are by contrast marked with energy and hopefulness. In R. W. Church's classic account, the mutual encouragement of Newman and his friends, bound together with the "affection characteristic of those days," was one of the principal causes of the heroic attempt to breathe new life into the Church of England. Newman's friendship with Froude was the deepest soil, a friendship that grew "in college out of unnoticed and unremembered talks, agreeing or differing, out of unconscious disclosures of temper and purpose, out of walks and rides and quiet breakfasts and common-room arguments, out of admirations and dislikes, out of letters and criticisms and questions." Close friendships like these are that "precious ointment on the head" (Ps. 132:2). Rare

---

52. See especially Marvin R. O'Connell, *The Oxford Conspirators: A History of the Oxford Movement* (New York: MacMillan, 1969).

53. John Henry Newman, *Sermons bearing on the Subjects of the Day* (London: Longmans, 1898), 409.

they are, and so mysteriously a gift that, again in Church's words, "nobody can tell afterwards how they have come about."[54]

If that friendship that rejoices in the truth is by nature a gift of divine grace, is it then foolhardy to think that a community of scholars might be animated with the kind of friendship that Newman and the leaders of the Oxford Movement enjoyed? Surely the experience of many in schools, colleges, and universities today would suggest that the groves of academe are among the thorniest, and as likely to produce enmity as charity. As with any spiritual good, however, the kind of friendship that consists in a shared pursuit of wisdom is both a gift and an ideal that can be striven for and even, to a degree, promoted by wise practices and sheltered by institutions. Newman, for one, seems to have remained sanguine about the possibilities for such fellow feeling to develop among scholars, penning a description of the university as an "assemblage of learned men, zealous for their own sciences, and rivals of each other [who] brought, by familiar intercourse and for the sake of intellectual peace, to adjust together the claims and relations of their respective subjects of investigation . . . learn to respect, to consult, to aid each other." "Thus is created," he concluded, "a pure and clear atmosphere of thought, which the student also breathes."[55] He was aware that institutional encouragement would be required to create the kind of academic fellowship he sought. Years earlier, when at Oriel, Newman had approached the formation of academic community with an awareness of the practices that such a community necessarily involved. One example of his activities comes from his tenure as dean at Oriel in the early 1830s, when he quarreled with the provost, Hawkins, over the admission of the gentleman commoners to the common room dinner table. Hawkins sided with the Oriel tradition of admitting these nonscholars; Newman pushed for their exclusion, so as to make the dinner table a privileged place of conversation for the Fellows. His motive in this attempt cannot be doubted. This was the same Newman whose influence with undergraduates had caused

---

54. Church, *Oxford Movement*, 27, 50.

55. *Idea of a University*, 76.

Hawkins's jealousy to flare. The privilege of common dining, for Newman, was not for its own sake, it was for the sake of that friendship among the Fellows which was the very model of the life that the students were to imitate.[56]

The college student's years of study take place during the season of life in which friendship is both most easily formed and most weighty in its consequences. It is precisely because the college is the stage on which the drama of friendship is enacted that it is able to become, as Newman put it, "the shrine of our best affections, the bosom of our fondest recollections, a spell upon our after life, a stay for world-weary mind and soul."[57] Teachers who find it difficult to cultivate friendship and practice it as a high ideal are unlikely to be able to understand, much less shape the lives of their students, whose collegiate lives are engulfed in friendship's concerns. If, however, the students' desire for friendship is nourished and directed by a compelling vision of the good life shown forth by their teachers' community, then the collegiate years may help to shape the balance of their adult lives for the better. Consider the example of Newman's imaginary contemporary, Edmund Bertram, who at a crucial moment early in *Mansfield Park* declared to the bewitching Mary Crawford that he had "not yet left Oxford long enough to forget what chapel prayers are."[58] Edmund's testimony was not to private piety, but to communal. In those days, chapel prayers were the corporate act of the Oxford College, in which "day by day memento [was] made," as Newman recollected, of the saving acts of God and of the ultimate destination of our intellectual life.[59] Yet chapel prayers cannot transform students if they are merely decorative. In order to inform the life of a college, the liturgy must be the crown laid upon a shared pursuit of wisdom and virtue by faculty and students. This pursuit cannot come about by ac-

---

56. See Culler, *Imperial Intellect*, 88.

57. *Rise and Progress of Universities*, 215.

58. Jane Austen, *Mansfield Park*, ed. James Kinsley (Oxford: Oxford University Press, 2003), 69.

59. *Idea of a University*, 117.

cident. If Christian wisdom is to be handed down to students, then it must first be chosen by the teachers, and to "rejoice in the truth" must be the common goal shaping the practices of the school.

The task facing American institutions of higher learning is, as Alasdair MacIntyre has declared, to recover "a less fragmented conception of what an education beyond high school should be."[60] Newman's collegiate ideal is anything but fragmented. Indeed, its unity in a bond of friendship seeking the truth, in the pastoral care for students, and in the rigorous teaching of elementary subjects may seem so foreign to us as to be undesirable. Yet it is the model that arises from our tradition.[61] Many centuries ago, Robert de Sorbon founded a college at the University of Paris with the help of his patron, St. Louis IX of France. Sorbon, loved by the king for his prudence, sought to frame an institution that could be a nourishing mother for young scholars. His rules make somewhat odd reading today, for they largely consist in minor regulations, many of which govern the taking of meals. Like St. Benedict before him, Sorbon wanted his scholars to live an orderly, quiet life and to share meals together, for that was the soil in which the highest of friendships could grow. After his death, the fellows of what became known as La Sorbonne distilled his teaching into their motto: *vivere socialiter, et collegialiter, et moraliter, et scholariter.*[62] The modern university can hardly imagine living by such a motto. The time would seem to be ripe, therefore, for the exploration of new institutional models to undertake the labor of translating Newman's collegiate ideal into a fitting and workable way of academic life that will serve the renewal of education in Christ.

---

60. Alasdair MacIntyre, "The End of Education: The Fragmentation of the American University," *Commonweal*, October 20, 2006, 10.

61. For two precursors to Newman's collegiate ideal, see Robert L. Wilken, "Alexandria: A School for Training in Virtue," in *Schools of Thought in the Christian Tradition*, ed. Patrick Henry (Philadelphia: Fortress Press, 1984), 15–30; and C. Stephen Jaeger, *The Envy of Angels: Cathedral School and Social Ideals in Medieval Europe, 950–1200* (Philadelphia: University of Pennsylvania Press, 1994).

62. P. Glorieux, *Aux origines de la Sorbonne, I. Robert de Sorbon* (Paris: J. Vrin, 1966), 42.

10

The Philosopher as Craftsman

AN ATTEMPT TO ELUCIDATE the educational ideal of one who has
declared that "any conception of the philosophy of education as a distinct area of philosophical enquiry is a mistake" must proceed with
caution.[1] Yet it ought to be made, for over the past half-century Alasdair MacIntyre has provided arguably the most trenchant and original commentary on education in the English language. The reason he
gave for his claim that there can be no independent philosophy of education—that "all teaching is for the sake of something else" and that
therefore "enquiries into education" are always a "part" of "enquiries
into the nature and goods of those activities into which we need to be
initiated by education"—is a principle that has animated his thoughts
on the subject since the 1950s.[2] Yet as his own conception of the human good has been progressively articulated, so also has the standard
to which he has held the role of the teacher and the institutions of
schools and universities. An examination of MacIntyre's writings on
education, therefore, promises to shed light on the broader tendencies
of his thinking. What may be more surprising, however, is to see the
way in which the end-point of the development of his thoughts on

---

1. Alasdair MacIntyre and Joseph Dunne, "Alasdair MacIntyre on Education: In
    Dialogue with Joseph Dunne," *Journal of the Philosophy of Education* 36 (2002): 1–19,
    at 9.

2. Ibid.

education represents a further extension of his response to the crisis of secular rationality.

MacIntyre has written memorable lines about the philosopher as a craftsman, and so it is fitting to attend to his discussions of the craft over the decades of his labor. From his participation in the New Left in the 1950s through his more recent writing as a Catholic and Thomist, he has consistently raised important theoretical issues while discussing the practices of the university life he has led. At the same time, his theoretical writings include many passing references to, as well as sustained treatments of, educational matters. Given the number of these passages, it will be necessary to choose a few as representative. Yet even these reveal the trajectory of his thought: from his early concern that the reform of educational institutions be a part of the quest for a just society, through the broader discussions of the role of higher education in the life of moral virtue during the middle decades of his career, to his growing appreciation of the speculative virtues in the last two decades of his life. Each stage in this development has involved a refining rather than an abandonment of his previous analysis, and the conclusion of it has been an integrated reflection upon the practices, virtues, institutional structures and communities that make possible the attainment of the highest of speculative virtues, wisdom. It is in MacIntyre's recent discussions of exemplars of a philosophical life that his treatment of education finds both its deepest significance and its greatest relevance to the malaise of secular modernity.

A Voice from the Moral Wilderness

One constant of Alasdair MacIntyre's career is certain: its moral seriousness. From the third decade of his life to the ninth, his writing has been characterized by an earnestness about the human good worthy of a Solzhenitsyn or a Wojtyla. As a committed Marxist, his reaction to the unmasking of Soviet tyranny in the 1950s was neither cynical nor romantic: it was to seek from the "moral wilderness" of his loss of confidence in communism a first principle sturdy enough to serve as the foundation of an ardent quest for the common good. Since at least 1956, he has robustly affirmed the priority of the common to the private or individual good, together with the truth that such a common good must be accessible to reason, indeed must be a good of reason.[3] His earliest discussions of education are in conformity with this principle and, like it, emerge from his opposition to classical liberalism. He insisted that the work of cultural criticism needed to remain "part of the political and industrial struggle," and, with other New Left writers, held that the "whole way of life which capitalism imposes" was the essential source of the moral failures of the age.[4] The necessary response was to struggle for a just society. "The philosophers," as he memorably put it, echoing Marx, "have continued to interpret the world differently; the point remains, to change it."[5]

MacIntyre's most sustained discussion of education from the 1950s, an essay entitled "Manchester: The Modern Universities and the English Tradition," was written with a reforming zeal to match his more overtly political essays. The concern that seems to have prompted the piece was a fear that the distinctive tradition of the provincial universities was soon to be eroded by the tide of incoming young faculty trained at Oxford and Cambridge who were not much inclined to respect the character of the institutions they were joining. Their unwillingness to think through the problems that these universities faced in light of the traditions proper to them had led to a "rash of Oxbridge solutions to Redbrick problems." MacIntyre found such proposals wanting: "To turn the provincial universities into residential institutions, to deplore specialist training and pine over some-

---

3. See MacIntyre, "Notes from the Moral Wilderness-II," *The New Reasoner* (1956), 96–97.

4. MacIntyre, "The 'New Left'," *Labour Review* 4 (1959): 99, 100. On MacIntyre's participation in the New Left, see Émile Perreau-Saussine, *Alasdair MacIntyre: une biographie intellectuelle. Introduction aux critiques contemporaines du libéralisme* (Paris: Presses Universitaires de France, 2005), 19–61.

5. MacIntyre, "Breaking the Chains of Reason," in *Out of Apathy*, ed. E. P. Thompson (London: Stevens, 1960), 240; with thanks to Professor Christopher Lutz for pointing out the connection to Marx.

thing called general education, to long for a tutorial system; this is to replace glorified technical colleges by rather inglorious imitations of Oxbridge."[6]

Worse than unrealistic, the attempt to imitate the ivy-covered colleges was the result of misaligned intention. Instead of a genuine spirit of service, these academics seemed chiefly to want to reproduce the trappings of a comfortable life of privilege. Speaking of these "immaculately attired young men on the teaching staff whose accents and umbrellas" signaled their pedigree, MacIntyre took a satirical turn: "After one has heard from them a dozen times how grossly inferior Manchester or Sheffield or Leeds is to Oxford or Cambridge one begins to weary of a nostalgia which is as inordinate as that of Ovid's Black Sea exile, but lacks all his elegiac charm." The sharpness of his rhetoric was proportionate to his concern that genuine goods were threatened. He admired the non-conformist tradition of English radical Protestantism, and spoke in praise of the "poetic standards of Watts and Wesley." And just as those Protestant traditions risked being contemptuously discarded, so also did the other great dissenting tradition of the British Isles risk having its character leached out in the acid-bath of affluence. English Roman Catholics, he warned, were all too likely to have "learned from . . . upper-class converts to seek an Oxbridge elegance."[7]

Against this danger, MacIntyre sought to defend what he called the "provincial tradition" of English university life. He identified four characteristics of this tradition, two of which—intellectual seriousness and liberalism—are not surprising. But two others are. He praised these institutions for having been "immersed in the life of local communities," a connection which helped to protect them from the creation of "an ingrown and hot-house social life." Again, there is a strong note of social critique in his account: "That one should not live on a campus or in a university town, but close to mills and factories

---

6. Alasdair MacIntyre, "Manchester: The Modern Universities and the English Tradition," *Twentieth Century* 159 (February 1956): 128.

7. Ibid., 123–25.

... is as good a way as any of preserving the university teacher from illusions about his place in society." The fourth characteristic was "a certain quality of thought" which he described as "an impatience with intellectual cant and with nonsense of all kinds," explaining what he meant in this paraphrase, "the contempt of the provincial for what he sees as the fripperies of aestheticism." What MacIntyre was most suspicious of was the elitism of the Oxbridge colleges, an elitism whose darker side he readily perceived, warning of "small collegiate communities" in which "it is easy for those with power to appoint like-minded people."[8] His indictment of the leading institutions of higher education in England was that they did not serve excellence and the common good so much as privilege and smug self-satisfaction.

In 1960, in another essay that addressed the topic, MacIntyre again sounded the note of class critique, making reference to an "American sociologist" who had "pictured our university teachers in a state of complacent delight, drinking port and reading Jane Austen" and jabbing at the "sweet smell of the academic's social success."[9] That essay, a jeremiad entitled "Breaking the Chains of Reason," bemoaned the complacency and irrelevance of academics and ascribed the apathy and conservatism of university scholars to their inability to affirm a substantive conception of human freedom based upon the exercise of reason. In an analysis that anticipated the central argument of *After Virtue*, he argued that capitalist society engenders habits of living and of thinking that mutually reinforce one another: "The vices of our lives and the errors of our concepts combine to keep both in being."[10] And because these vices are inculcated by the power structures of capitalist society, the attempt to fix habits of thought by themselves will be futile: "you can only carry through any effective educational effort as part of the political and industrial struggle."[11]

---

8. Ibid., 126–27.

9. MacIntyre, "Breaking the Chains of Reason," in *Out of Apathy*, ed. E. P. Thompson (London: Stevens, 1960), 195–96.

10. Ibid., 231.

11. "The 'New Left,'" 100.

Communities of Virtue

Whether or not MacIntyre's immigration to America should be taken to represent his coming to terms with the structures of liberal democracy, his active participation in left-wing politics did come to an end with the tumultuous 1960s.[12] During the 1970s, his great labor was one of intellectual conversion, documented in the pages of *After Virtue*. In addition to being a strikingly original work of moral philosophy, that book is also in important respects an example of confessional literature, and the conversion that it documents is one that brought MacIntyre to differ with his own previous academic life and so, necessarily, with the practices and institutions of the modern academy generally. The crucial difference is that whereas MacIntyre had earlier criticized university life as symptomatic of the cultural ills of capitalism, in *After Virtue* the modern university is singled out as a contributing cause of the misunderstanding of the moral life and, consequently, a barrier to be overcome if both the theory and the life of the virtues were to be regained. Over the next decade and a half, he would elaborate an alternative vision of university life that is at once a response to a crisis in the academy but also a part—and perhaps even a necessary one—of the moral regeneration of society.

MacIntyre's essential claim about education in *After Virtue* has lost none of its ability to surprise with the passage of thirty years: that the form taken by our academic life prevents us from rightly understanding the character of our age. The transition to modernity that he understands as a loss of the tradition of the virtues is one that is "invisible" from the value-neutral "standpoint of academic history." Moreover, the "habits of mind engendered by our modern academic curriculum" make it difficult, if not impossible, to see the connection between conceptual and social changes—shifts in our way of thinking and in our patterns of life. In view here is the habitual compartmentalization, or, as he put it, "the tendency to think atomistically about human action," that characterizes not only our moral lives in general,

---

12. See Perreau-Saussine, *Alasdair MacIntyre*, 47–61.

but our academic institutions and practices as well.[13] Philosophy, from having been the common habit of reasoning possessed by an entire educated public, has become a highly circumscribed and narrowly professional pursuit.[14] Not only is philosophy cut off from life, it is even rigidly separated from subjects that either should be closely annexed to it or, arguably, should be thought of as its own subordinate parts, such as the sociology of morals. This artificial curricular division— the product of professionalization—itself reproduces the essential ways in which modernity earlier broke with traditional society and the morality of the virtues that enlivened it: by rejecting the broadly speaking Aristotelian conception of man as having both a nature and a function within a larger social whole. In MacIntyre's own words, "the disjunctions and divorces of the eighteenth century perpetuate and reinforce themselves in contemporary curricular divisions."[15]

The solution to the ills of modernity that MacIntyre proposed at the end of *After Virtue* is well-known. Yet it may not have been sufficiently realized just how central to his conception of a community of virtue is the role of teacher and the institution that is the school. The very choice of St. Benedict as his archetypal exemplar did point in that direction, for Benedict famously called the monastery a "school for the Lord's service" and understood the mutual teaching of the brother monks to be an essential part of their quest for virtuous living. MacIntyre himself subsequently stressed that all of the virtues "have to be developed throughout one's entire life" and that our quest for happiness must be understood as "a lifelong process of learning and imparting truths," a process that unfolds in a context of "mutual relationships of teaching and learning."[16] The school, then, and the

---

13. *After Virtue: A Study in Moral Theory*, 3rd edition (1981; Notre Dame, IN: University of Notre Dame Press, 2006), quotations from 4, 61, and 204.

14. See *After Virtue*, 50–51, and his subsequent elaboration of this point in "The Idea of an Educated Public," in *Education and Values: The Richard Peters Lectures*, ed. Graham Haydon (London: University of London Institute of Education, 1987), 15–36.

15. *After Virtue*, 72–73 and 82.

16. MacIntyre, "The Privatization of Good: An Inaugural Lecture," *Review of Politics* 52 (1990): 358.

student-teacher relationship, turn out to be places where the pursuit of virtue is condensed and, as it were, crystallized. If we ought to consider our lives as a whole as being a kind of education, then it seems fitting that we consider our formal education as essentially serving that larger and more universal pursuit of the good. Educational practices and institutions, therefore, not only provide evidence or symptoms of our success or failure in the pursuit of virtue, they are microcosms and the crucial test-cases of that pursuit.[17]

Nowhere does MacIntyre's earnestness about education impress itself upon the reader more than in his inaugural lecture at the University of Notre Dame on "The Privatization of Good." Essential to the task of refuting secular liberalism in its various guises is the witness of a successful pursuit of the traditional virtues. The claim made by the traditional theory of the virtues, after all, is not merely that it manages to avoid contradicting itself, but also that, if the theory be followed, it will in fact result in a tolerable approximation of the good life. This is why, as MacIntyre put it: "the strengths of an Aristotelian and Thomistic position will only become clear insofar as it too is seen to be embodied in particularized forms of practice."[18] Having sounded this note, he closed the lecture by challenging his audience to join him in the attempt to make the academic community at Notre Dame provide in its common life compelling evidence of the truth that men and women are perfected by the virtues as traditionally understood. The passage is more than a little poignant: "as to that remaking of ourselves and our own local practices and institutions through a better understanding of what it is that, in an Aristotelian and Thomistic

---

17. Thus, presumably, his readiness to address the concerns of teachers and teachers themselves. See, for instance, his "Traditions and Conflicts," *Liberal Education* 73 (1987): 6–13; "How to Be a North American," a lecture presented at the National Conference of State Humanities Councils (Washington, DC: Federation of State Humanities Councils, 1987); and "How Is Intellectual Excellence in Philosophy to Be Understood by a Catholic Philosopher? What Has Philosophy to Contribute to Catholic Intellectual Excellence?," *Current Issues in Catholic Higher Education* 12 (1991): 47–50.

18. "The Privatization of Good," 360.

perspective, the unity of moral theory and practice now require of us, we have as much to hope for as we have to do, and not least within the community of this university."[19]

Overshadowed by MacIntyre's striking conception of a university as a battleground upon which competing traditions fight for the mastery, a conception developed in his *Three Rival Versions of Moral Enquiry* (1990), the aspiration this passage expresses has been overlooked. Yet its significance within the course of his thinking should not be minimized, for if the tragedy of secular reason and the failure of the Enlightenment project have come about because of the progressive instantiation in social forms of a shift in philosophical principles, it seems reasonable to suppose that the shift back to an Aristotelian way of thinking and living could be accomplished best—and perhaps even first—in a college or university, precisely because a school is the kind of institution in which principles and practices can and ought to be most closely harmonized. It is this aspiration which makes sense of the tenor of much of his subsequent commentary on higher education.[20] The inability of the contemporary Catholic university to reverse the trend of the fragmentation of curricula and the narrow focus of undergraduate education upon preparedness for professional life—even, and perhaps especially, in the humanities—is nothing less than a tragedy because of the high promise of a well-thought-out and well-run educational institution: the formation of its students for lives of creative and trustworthy practical judgment about weighty matters.[21]

---

19. Ibid., 361.

20. Even if perhaps expressed somewhat diffidently in his "Aquinas's Critique of Education: Against His Own Age, Against Ours," in *Philosophers on Education: Historical Perspectives*, Amélie Oksenberg Rorty, ed. (London: Routledge, 1998), 95–108.

21. See "Catholic Universities: Dangers, Hopes, Choices," in *Higher Learning and Catholic Traditions*, Robert E. Sullivan, ed. (Notre Dame, IN: University of Notre Dame Press, 2001), 1–21, but also, and with greater insistence, his "The End of Education: The Fragmentation of the American University," *Commonweal* (October 20, 2006), 10–14, and more recently, "The Very Idea of a University: Aristotle, Newman, and Us," *British Journal of Educational Studies* 57 (2009): 347–62.

Exemplary Philosophical Lives

By comparison to the prophetic tone of *After Virtue* and the high seriousness of the vision of intellectual combat offered in *Three Rival Versions of Moral Enquiry*, one is struck by what Reinhard Hütter described as the "disquieting, not to say despairing" tone of MacIntyre's *God, Philosophy, Universities*.[22] On the subject of education, the volume appears to mark a decisive retreat from his earlier thought. It is, after all, a frankly professional model of philosophy that he discusses at the book's end, which, though tempered by his discussion of John Paul II's *Fides et Ratio* and his insistence that philosophy find both its origin and its destination in the questions asked by us all as "plain persons," nevertheless seems much less idealistic than his earlier contributions. At the level of controlling metaphor, it is one thing to be imitating St. Benedict, quite another to bring a sweeping narrative of the history of philosophy to an end by tacitly recommending an apprenticeship to one who is most assuredly a philosopher's philosopher, Elizabeth Anscombe.[23] Such a retreat, moreover, would even seem to be a confirmed fact about the latter MacIntyre. For, on the face of it, to suggest that "perhaps the point of doing philosophy is to enable people to lead, so far as it is within their powers, philosophical lives," as he did in an essay published in 2006, seems to be worlds apart from his earlier rallying cry, "the philosophers have continued to interpret the world differently; the point remains, to change it."[24] An emphasis on the practical living out of philosophical convictions remains, to be sure, but his focus seems now to be decisively private and personal. Yet the retreat

---

22. Reinhard Hütter, "Seeking Truth on Dry Soil and under Thornbushes—God, the University, and the Missing Link: Wisdom," in his *Dust Bound for Heaven: Explorations in the Theology of Thomas Aquinas* (Grand Rapids, MI: Eerdmans, 2012), 392.

23. See *God, Philosophy, Universities: A Selective History of the Catholic Philosophical Tradition* (Lanham, MD: Rowman and Littlefield, 2009), 160–62.

24. MacIntyre, "The Ends of Life, the Ends of Philosophical Writing," in his *The Tasks of Philosophy: Selected Essays, Volume 1* (Cambridge: Cambridge University Press, 2006), 132; the earlier statement is from his "Breaking the Chains of Reason," cited above in note 5.

is merely apparent, and when *God, Philosophy, Universities* is placed in a broader context, its true significance can be better appreciated.

A work that should be considered if one is to understand the latter MacIntyre is his philosophical biography of the young Edith Stein. What upon first reading may seem to be merely the report of a difficult bout of wrestling with phenomenology is in fact also a dramatic narrative of the pursuit of truth within the context of the modern university. At the heart of MacIntyre's story is the life, death, and philosophical inquiry of Stein's mentor and friend Adolf Reinach. Like other talented young philosophers of his generation—such as Max Scheler and Dietrich von Hildebrand—Reinach had come to Göttingen to learn from Edmund Husserl. Yet this was no easy task. Husserl's prickly and abstracted character was, to a degree, smoothed out and compensated for by his wife, but his students do not seem to have been really comfortable with him. They called him "the Master," feared disagreements with him, and learned to lower their expectations of his hospitality. The forbidding role of the Professor in those days was only one of the challenges of German academic culture; Stein's colleagues and fellow-students were also at times a cause of grief. MacIntyre writes of the "tiresome vanity" of Scheler, gently points out the rudeness of another member of the Husserl circle by saying that the "focused intensity of his conversational manner sometimes alienated listeners," and sums up the misanthropy of Martin Heidegger by explaining that after he left the Husserl circle, he entered into "relationships only with those who [were] prepared to acknowledge his superiority."[25]

Adolf Reinach, to the contrary, was a model of the virtues necessary for the successful pursuit and sharing of truth. Both Reinach and his wife Anna were unstinting with the gift of their friendship, a gift which the young Edith Stein found especially valuable. Reinach, moreover, was known for his patient, teacherly expositions of Husserl's turgid thought. He was generous with his time and encourag-

---

25. MacIntyre, *Edith Stein: A Philosophical Prologue, 1913–1922* (Lanham, MD: Rowman & Littlefield, 2006), quotations from pages 67, 90, 103, and 185.

ing with his advice. And, crucially, Reinach understood and practiced philosophy as a "cooperative enterprise," as MacIntyre puts it. The academic life pursued by Adolf Reinach, Edith Stein, and a few others during the early 1910s in Göttingen was a common life of friendship in pursuit of truth. Although the friendships were not destined to be prolonged into a happy old age, they did much to shape the lives of those who enjoyed them. Reinach, a dutiful subject of the Kaiser, went off to the Great War, won the Iron Cross, and was killed in action. But not before he had been baptized a Christian. He took with him to the front his New Testament, the *Imitation of Christ*, and Augustine's *Confessions*. From this spare but deep reading, he nourished his reflection upon his own personal experiences of God in prayer, leaving behind notes for a book on faith and reason. Writing to his wife from the front, he testified to his conviction that this inquiry was crucial: "To do such work with humility is most important today, far more important than to fight this war. For what purpose has this horror if it does not lead human beings closer to God?"[26]

In addition to his own noble death, Reinach bequeathed to Edith Stein an example of the serious and disinterested pursuit of truth that made it possible for her to choose a path in life that led—so far as these things can be judged by outsiders—to a high degree of rational contentment. In place of the alienating and frustrating experiences of the German university system, she enjoyed a fruitful career as a secondary school teacher and part-time catechist and apologist for the Catholic faith, before joining the Carmelite order and pursuing her philosophical and theological studies with renewed vigor. Although it may require the perspective of faith in order fully to apprehend the nobility of her death and thus to be able to see her life as a successful and integrated whole, the more modest conclusions that MacIntyre offers in his study of her early life are readily appreciable. He takes the silence that followed her conversion to Christianity as an especially important sign. Unlike other philosophical conversions that he discusses, Stein's seems incontestably to have brought about a deep

---

26. *Edith Stein: A Philosophical Prologue*, quotations from pages 139 and 146.

satisfaction of mind, even a peace, which manifested itself first by years of quiet thoughtfulness and subsequently by her ability to give of herself generously to the community in which the truth she had been seeking—the truth about God—found a home.[27]

The lasting or deepest significance of *Edith Stein: A Philosophical Prologue* within MacIntyre's corpus of work, then, may not be in its discussion of phenomenology, but instead in the way it provides a kind of completion to his discussions of education. The reforming zeal he had displayed in the 1950s has not been entirely lost here; indeed, he forthrightly portrays the failures of the German university system. The earnest seeker of truth that was Edith Stein did not find a lasting home at Göttingen, but instead in a Carmelite convent. With this story, MacIntyre offers an understated proposal that is just as important as his hope for a new St. Benedict or his defense of Manchester University, for Stein's life as a religious sister who wrote philosophical and theological works is an example of service to the truth every bit as eloquent as these earlier ones.

Yet there is another and still more important dimension to MacIntyre's *Edith Stein* and his recent essays touching on education, and that is his increasing confidence in metaphysical affirmation. The trajectory of his metaphysical convictions may be rapidly sketched. In the 1950s and 1960s, although reading deeply in metaphysics, he nevertheless wrote as a reporter and a critic.[28] His discussions of education terminate with moral truths and social facts: his chief concern is not that undergraduates are failing to learn their proofs for the ex-

---

27. On Stein's silence, see *Edith Stein: A Philosophical Prologue*, 172–73. For MacIntyre's treatment of philosophical conversions, see chapter 15 of the same volume, and also his essay covering much of the same ground, "The Ends of Life, the Ends of Philosophical Writing."

28. See, for instance, his "Analogy in Metaphysics," *Downside Review* 69 (1950): 45–61, and "Being," *Encyclopedia of Philosophy*, ed. Paul Edwards (New York: Macmillan, 1967), I:273–77. It could be that his early convictions would be qualified as not merely detached from but positively negative about the possibility of traditional metaphysics. See his "A Society without a Metaphysics," *The Listener* (September 13, 1956), 376: "to anyone working within contemporary philosophy it must be clear that the old metaphysical Absolutes are dead beyond recovery."

istence of God, but rather that they are being habituated for a life as upper–middle-class consumers of luxury goods. In the 1980s and 1990s, MacIntyre's analysis goes further. The essential failure of the modern university is that it deforms not only the social aspirations of the students but the practical intellect itself. The fragmentation of the curriculum mirrors and reinforces the compartmentalization of life, and the end result of this must sooner or later be tragic.[29] Beginning in the 1990s, however, MacIntyre more and more robustly affirms propositions about the natures of things, beginning with the nature of man as a reasoning animal, but then more and more explicitly and insistently, propositions about truth and God.[30] His increasing attention to prior and more universal causes goes along with an increasing insistence about the guiding principle of education. It is in the context of this trajectory that *God, Philosophy, Universities* should be read, not as a retreat, but as a fresh start.[31] One ought to marvel at a philosopher in the evening of his life attempting such an endeavor, his earlier career having been so different, and even in important respects at variance with it. MacIntyre's address at the annual meeting of the American Catholic Philosophical Association in 2011, "How to Be a Theistic Philosopher in a Secularized Culture," brings the development of his thought about education to a kind of apogee with the statement that the difference between a theist and an atheist is not merely what they say about God, but what they say about everything else. "To be a theist," he explains, "is to understand every particular as, by reason of its finitude and its contingency, pointing towards God." To be a theist, accordingly, is "to hold that all explanation and understanding that does

---

29. In addition to the essays cited above in notes 17 and 21, see his "Social Structures and their Threat Moral Agency," *Philosophy* 74 (1999): 311–29.

30. In addition to his *Dependent Rational Animals: Why Human Beings Need the Virtues* (Peru, IL: Open Court, 1999), one ought to note the essays "What Is a Human Body?" and "Truth as a Good: A Reflection on *Fides et Ratio*," both included in *The Tasks of Philosophy*.

31. For such a reading, see Hütter's essay, cited above in note 22, especially pages 392 and 402–3.

not refer us to God both as first cause and as final end is incomplete."[32] This search for satisfactory explanations not only divides the theistic from the secular philosopher, but it also has important ramifications for education.

A Response to the Secular Mind

One may well ask just what sort of secular mind MacIntyre has in view by his division between the theistic and the atheistic philosopher. After all, the Stephen Weinbergs of the world do not seem to be lacking in their search for ever more capacious and powerful explanations. In the essay at hand, MacIntyre quite rightly responds to the physicalist reductionism that characterizes much contemporary atheism. Yet one may also observe that the ironic detachment exemplified by Richard Rorty seems to be just as characteristic of the secular mind, if not more so. For the closing off of systematic inquiry into causes seems much more likely to take place today at an earlier moment, long before quantum fields have been reached. Rorty's astonishing assertion that it is literary criticism rather than philosophy that is the governing discourse—and his equally if not more astonishing display of philosophy as a kind of story-telling—does seem an accurate assessment of both our common culture and, in a certain sense, the academy as well.[33] Rorty's concern was to discover what effactully moves us to adopt a more tolerant attitude toward other men and women; his conviction is that the reading of novels and even the watching of movies and television shows today supplies the fuel for moral conviction that in the past was provided by philosophical conviction or religious belief. But his assessment, of course, applies more broadly. In Rorty's pragmatism, practical judgments seem to rest not so much upon utility or profit or the avoidance of pain, but upon aesthetic sensibilities and passions.

---

32. MacIntyre, "On Being a Theistic Philosopher in a Secularized Culture," *Proceedings of the ACPA* 84 (2011): 23.

33. See Richard Rorty, *Contingency, Irony, and Solidarity* (Cambridge: Cambridge University Press, 1989).

And this is why he seems indeed to have captured the secular mind almost perfectly—much like David Hume before him. For today, our mental preoccupations seem more than ever to rise from our changing desires as consumers of cultural products, whether those products be made in Hollywood or by a university press.

Why is MacIntyre's insistence that the theistic philosopher ought relentlessly to pursue the task of explanation until he has arrived at the consideration of the first cause and final end so important? Because the alternative to it is the suave sophistry of our age, in which communities of discourse limited to matters of narrow scope threaten to stultify our pursuit of truth and the mental lives of our students. Just as in the case of Protagoras of old, the personal charm, ready wit, and moral authority conferred by success and rank that were enjoyed by Rorty himself and are shared by many academics today are qualities capable of generating a subculture—or even a dominant culture—that is almost impervious to critique. Socrates plainly thought that he needed to proceed to the drastic step of drinking the hemlock in order to convince friends like Crito that the rational life of the virtues was better than the life of pleasure. And, to recall MacIntyre's own examples, for Adolph Reinach, the experience of war seems to have been crucial in deepening his quest for truth, while for Edith Stein, Reinach's death and his wife's acceptance of it were the essential witnesses.

Yet what does all of this have to do with education? Precisely this: the culture of higher education—and this is increasingly true of secondary education as well—has been shaped by the Rortys of our day. The result has been a retreat into a professional mode of philosophizing in which the work of many of us is characterized by overly nice distinctions, an insistence upon apparatus over argument, and an overall soft skepticism in which affirmation is undervalued and politeness to interlocutors overvalued. These habits are chiefly to be seen in the writing and speaking of our professional lives, but they also have a way of making themselves felt in curricular discussions and even the grading of student papers. This is why more and more voices are warning that the intellectual life is being dissolved into mere professionalism.[34] The challenge of affirming that, in the last analysis, it is the knowledge of God that perfects the human intellect is a test that is being failed even by philosophers and theologians of unimpeachable Christian seriousness.[35] But short of an earnest attempt to make the difficult ascent toward the affirmation of propositions about things we cannot see—the virtues, the natures of things, truth, and God—we will not be able to put our educational practices and institutions into any satisfactory order.

And so, by proposing as models Anscombe and John Paul II, Edith Stein and Adolf Reinach, Alasdair MacIntyre has at once offered a vision of academic life as well as a response to contemporary secularism. Against the self-satisfied and resolute aestheticism that takes any intellectual inquiry to be good so long as there is someone to desire it and insists that these intellectual goods have no order among them, MacIntyre has argued for a deeply purposeful approach to the life of the mind.[36] Yet perhaps just as crucially, he has exempli-

---

34. See, for instance, Bernard Williams, *Truth and Truthfulness: An Essay in Genealogy* (Princeton: Princeton University Press, 2002), 3: "[A]t the present time, the study of the humanities runs a risk of sliding from professional seriousness, through professionalization, to a finally disenchanted careerism."

35. For instance, Robert C. Roberts and W. Jay Wood, *Intellectual Virtues: An Essay in Regulative Epistemology* (New York: Oxford University Press, 2007), 180: "We have to reckon with the possibility that what some serious people take to be knowledge is not knowledge, and that what some people take to be intellectual virtues are not virtues," but the matter "could be decided only by a sort of metaphysical adjudication which is in all probability unavailable to human beings." And, in a different key, but to a similar end, Paul J. Griffiths, *Intellectual Appetite: A Theological Grammar* (Washington, DC: Catholic University of America Press, 2009), 111: "There is, however, no single, obvious, compelling taxonomic ordering of appetites: any particular ordering depends on and is deeply articulated with local catechesis."

36. See, on this point, the whole of his "Truth as a Good: A Reflection upon *Fides et Ratio*," in *The Tasks of Philosophy*, but especially this formulation of the typical stance of contemporary academics with respect to intellectual goods, at 208: "if we lacked any conception of such an absolute standpoint, we might well conclude that there is no such thing as a final terminus for enquiry concerning any particular subject matter. What directs enquiry on this alternative view are whatever may happen to be our explanatory interests and in taking this or that as the goal

fied it in his own philosophical life. Broad in his interests from the beginning of his career, he did most rigorously pursue his particular craft, moral philosophy; *After Virtue* will continue to be read as long as moral philosophy is studied in the English-speaking world. By committing him to the defense of a tradition of inquiry encompassing more than ethics, that work led him to tackle progressively more capacious questions, and led him eventually to the philosophy of nature and metaphysics. As anyone conversant with his career can validate, MacIntyre is no dabbler: it is plain that he has been following out a line of inquiry with energy and skill. The virtue that has shaped that inquiry is his openness to consider difficulties with respect to progressively prior principles and, accordingly, progressively broader explanations. This openness is the precise opposite to the premature closure upon questioning that is seen in Rorty's prescription that we ought simply to accept as boundaries the sensibilities that history has bequeathed to us. In contrast to that anti-philosophical orientation, MacIntyre's life of inquiry is characterized by the relentlessness of a quest. His questions have deepened and broadened, from "What does justice require?" to "What sort of life will make me happy?" to "What sort of being am I?" to "What is truth?" and, finally, to Aquinas's question, "What is God?"

It is because of his fearless pursuit of truth that MacIntyre is the great craftsman-philosopher of our age. As his biographer, the late Émile Perreau-Saussine, aptly said, although MacIntyre was initially "carried away by the political passions of his century," in his later life he "progressively rediscovered wisdom."[37] He is like a furniture-maker who was trained to make chairs and then worried, and sweated, and toiled to make better ones, and succeeded. But then, instead of seeking only to profit from his chairs, he looked abroad and saw that in the making of chests further excellences remained for him to seek.

---

of enquiry in some particular area we are only giving expression to our interests as they happen to be now, but may not be in the future, interests that may also differ from social group to social group."

37. Perreau-Saussine, *Alasdair MacIntyre*, 163.

So he acquired new tools, learned to use them, and made new works. He remains known for his chairs, chairs that have only improved because of his work on more difficult pieces. Yet he should especially be celebrated for his love for the craft, for he has exemplified the pursuit of the full excellence it offers. And, in the case of Alasdair MacIntyre, the craft he has shown us how to practice is the craft of crafts, the most human of arts, the art of thinking. In an address to his fellow artisans, he suggested that "what we need now are thinkers who combine philosophical acumen and argument with the wit of Chesterton and the satire of Waugh."[38] Could it not rather be said that the quality we—and our students—need first is the thirst for truth of Alasdair MacIntyre?

---

38. MacIntyre, "On Being a Theistic Philosopher," 32.

Index

Acknowledgments of Previous Publication

THE AUTHOR GRATEFULLY ACKNOWLEDGES the following journals and reviews for having published earlier versions of these essays and for allowing their republication here.

Chapter 1. "Where Is the Wisdom We Have Lost in Knowledge?: The Cultural Tragedy of the Enlightenment," *Downside Review* 125 (January 2007).

Chapter 2. "The Studiousness of Jacques-Bénigne Bossuet," *Nova et Vetera*, English edition 8 (2010).

Chapter 3. "A Fruitful Restraint: The Perennial Relevance of the Virtue of Studiousness," *Nova et Vetera*, English edition 11 (2013).

Chapter 4. "On the Recovery of Experience and the Search for a Christian Environmentalism," *Nova et Vetera*, English edition 10 (2012).

Chapter 5. "The Beauty of Reasoning: Considerations on Book V of Euclid's *Elements*," *Aquinas Review* 15 (2009).

Chapter 7. "The Historian and His Tools in the Workshop of Wisdom," Logos 13 (2010).

Chapter 8. "The Prospect of an Aristotelian Biology," *Proceedings of the American Catholic Philosophical Association* 87 (2013).

Chapter 9. "Newman's Collegiate Ideal," *Pro Ecclesia*, 17 (2008).

Chapter 10. "The Craftsman's Tools: MacIntyre on Education," *Nova et Vetera*, English edition 12 (2014).

Acknowledgments

ONE OF THE ESSENTIAL lessons of life surely is that the Lord of Mercy often answers our prayers through the mediation of other people. Accordingly, for whatever measure of wisdom has been granted to me, I have many friends to thank.

Always first are Kathleen, John, and Isabel, whose patience and love are life to me.

We four have been blessed to share our lives and labors with some very dear families over the past two decades in three remarkable academic communities. On behalf of my family, then, I would express our affectionate gratitude to the Andres, Benischek, Brown, Cuddeback, Fahey, Reyes, Soutsos, Nelson, McKinney, Thompson, Dalton, Gray, Logan, and Sri families.

My sincere thanks also to the many students—too numerous to begin naming here—whose contributions to this volume have been essential.

These essays that have coalesced into an argument about a certain kind of academic life have been by turns inspired, encouraged, and criticized by many friends and mentors, including: Tony Andres, Mike Augros, James Barham, Don Briel, John Boyle, Douglas Bushman, Rev. Romanus Cessario, O.P., Matthew Levering, Reinhard Hütter, V. Bradley Lewis, Tom McLaughlin, Rev. Wilson Miscamble, C.S.C., John Francis Nieto, Rev. Marvin O'Connell, Christopher

Shannon, Phillip R. Sloan, and Robert Louis Wilken. I am deeply grateful for their learning and goodness.

Finally, I am bound to express my great debt to two wise men whose insights and example have been central to the whole of this book—Walter J. Thompson and the Rev. Michael J. Keating—and to the teacher who has long exemplified for me both fearlessness in the pursuit of wisdom and generosity in the disinterested communication of truth, Michael D. Aeschliman.